The Southern Poetry Anthology
Volume I: South Carolina

The Southern Poetry Anthology
Volume I: South Carolina

Edited by

Stephen Gardner and William Wright

Texas Review Press
Huntsville, Texas

FIRST EDITION, 2007

Requests for permission to reproduce material from this work should be sent to:

Permissions
Texas Review Press
English Department
Sam Houston State University
Huntsville, TX 77341-2146

Cover photo by David Lewiston, Henreitta Yurchenko Collection, American Folklife
Center, Library of Congress

Library of Congress Cataloging-in-Publication Data

The Southern poetry anthology : South Carolina / [compiled] by Stephen Gardner and
William Wright. ~ 1st ed.
    p. cm.
  ISBN-13: 978-1-933896-06-9 (pbk. : alk. paper)
  ISBN-10: 1-933896-06-X (pbk. : alk. paper)
  1. American poetry~South Carolina. I. Gardner, Stephen. II. Wright, William,
1979-
  PS558.S6S68 2007
  811.008'09757~dc22
                         2007023711

The Southern Poetry Anthology
Volume I: South Carolina

EDITORS' INTRODUCTION

What follows here is a cautionary tale.

It has to do with answering a ringing phone, late at night, alone, two shots toward an early morning.

It has to do with a former-student-turned friend who is less than half one's age and who, therefore, is endowed with more energy and excitement and ideas.

It has to do with the inability to say no, contrary to whatever common sense that might have been bestowed upon a stone.

One of us had the notion; the other had reservations but lacked the ability to decline. It was, after all, a really good idea. But the caution: Leave the ringing to die on its own.

You have before you the consequences of that conversation, concocted and consummated after just over two years of sowing, tending, and reaping. Our premise—the idea—is simple. Start with South Carolina, our native turf, where we know many writers, and make an anthology of contemporary poets who have some connection with the state. All that we required was that submissions be from poets who are native South Carolinians or who have lived, now or in the past, in the state for at least one year. We did not limit the anthology to works that had been, or had not been, previously published. We did stipulate that poets had to possess the rights to the poems or be able to secure those rights. We encouraged submissions from established writers as well as those who had not been published. We were open to both formal poems and free verse, the traditional and experimental. As we stated in our submission guidelines, our only serious rule was that, in order to be selected, the poems had to be "original and of high quality."

Make an anthology. An anthology that will be the first of a series, state by state, covering the South. Piece of literary cake. We know Texas. Know Mississippi, Virginia. Georgia. Alabama, Louisiana, Tennessee. All the rest, even reaching into the "Border States." Let's see: At a mere two years per volume, one of us will be thinking about retirement; the other, dirt-bound (or urn-bound) and hoping for Resurrection.

It remains to be seen what we might have learned from this project, what might occur next. But this is what we have done, and this is where we are.

There will be people angry, those who know that they should be in here but are not. We reached out every way that we knew how: statewide newspapers, mailed calls for manuscripts, notices to societies, word of mouth. We made direct appeals to many poets; some, for reasons known only to themselves, elected not to reply, even to multiple pleadings. We regret their absence here, but that choice was theirs. Some contacted us; but, after that contact, they failed to deliver the goods. Some small, rare few were unwilling (or, giving the best thought to the matter, unable) for whatever reason to provide us with necessary information concerning copyright ownership and/or notice of previous publication. We regret the absence of all of these people, because we know that their presence in this, our first house, would have ennobled the hearth table.

But we believe, and we fervently hope that you will concur, that the assemblage between these covers is a hearty lot, a lusty lot, a crew of disparate voices sloshing their literary ale and singing old bards' songs beneath a ceiling of timbers so that the raw rafters echo with a cacophony turned beautiful.

Perhaps it is good to pick up that telephone. Perhaps it is good to say yes.

South Carolina down, somewhere else to go.

We also gratefully thank the following who, in one way (or in multiple ways) or another have assisted in bringing this anthology to life:

Chancellor Thomas Hallman and Executive Vice Chancellor for Academic Affairs Suzanne Ozment of the University of South Carolina Aiken, for their support of this project;

The Aiken Partnership and the G. L. Toole Chair Endowment, for providing fiscal resources;

Dr. Paul Ruffin and the staff at Texas Review Press, for their willingness to believe and to trust us to prestidigitate this volume into being and for being financial partners in the process;

Henrietta Yurchenco, David Lewiston, Ann Hoog, and the Library of Congress for the use of the cover photograph;

Our friends and students and loved ones who endured, with grace and understanding, the occasional slight or edginess when the work sometimes turned to burden instead of the normal pleasure;

Josephine Biga and Michelle Nichols, for their assistance with files, proofreading, and the ancillary arts of keeping people on track when the track appears impassible or just no longer quite worth the effort;

James Howell for significant aid in the design of the cover;

And these seventy-six gifted writers included herein, for honoring us with the permission to reproduce their work and to present it to you.

Stephen L. Gardner, Aiken, SC
William G. Wright, Hattiesburg, MS

Table of Contents

The Southern Poetry Anthology
Volume I: South Carolina

DAN ALBERGOTTI

The Chiming of the Hour

The low tone of heavy December wind
moving through the attic's slatted vents
awakens the woman lying on her side.
She sees how the muted morning light
drifts through window blinds and how her husband,
who was alive in her dream, is again in the earth.
This is the gray day that the Lord hath made.
She hears the soft, rapid ticking of the clock
beside her bed and how it mingles with
the bells outside. The woman does not know
why the wind chimes sound altogether different
in winter months. She does not know
what puts her in her navy dress and heels,
behind the wheel of her husband's old car,
and in the pew they sat in all those years.
But she stands with the parishioners and mouths
the words of the doxology, her whisper lost
in the throng. She sits back down with them.
Back home, she will read the bulletin
and listen to the cable news anchorman
as if he were a bothersome neighbor child.
She does not know why again she will not
clean the tables and mantelpiece of the gathering dust
nor why she has to check each windup clock
before she puts herself back into the dark.
Sometimes she wakes up singing.

Revision

After two weeks under the Italian sun,
he would dash off a note to Fanny Brawne:
"Weather marvelous. Fully recovered.
Come soon and bring summer dresses."
And she would come. She would pull
his miraculous heart to her breast,
and they would listen to every bird's song.
The odes would win a silly contest,
and they would use the prize money
to build a small house on a Greek island.
They would spend the next twenty years
perfecting the art of the human body.
They would eat fine olives and swallow
the sound of each wave's roll onto the beach.
They would make love under the night sky
with such tense clarity that the moon
would become the bright face of God.
One morning the man would pick up his pen,
sit by the window, write, "I was happy
to be John Keats," and never write again.

Things to Do in the Belly of the Whale

Measure the walls. Count the ribs. Notch the long days.
Look up for blue sky through the spout. Make small fires
with the broken hulls of fishing boats. Practice smoke signals.
Call old friends, and listen for echoes of distant voices.
Organize your calendar. Dream of the beach. Look each way
for the dim glow of light. Work on your reports. Review
each of your life's ten million choices. Endure moments
of self-loathing. Find the evidence of those before you.
Destroy it. Try to be very quiet, and listen for the sound
of gears and moving water. Listen for the sound of your heart.
Be thankful that you are here, swallowed with all hope,
where you can rest and wait. Be nostalgic. Think of all
the things you did and could have done. Remember
treading water in the center of the still night sea, your toes
pointing again and again down, down into the black depths.

GILBERT ALLEN

The Noah of Travelers Rest

You could see his vessel
from Highway 25, keel foundering
on land cursed with kudzu and God knew
what creeping within it.

He'd built his defiance fifty feet long
in the trough between
two waves of mountains, prow
pointed toward sunset, and waited

for rain—which came, and went, and came
again—but never enough to make
even a spouse entertain the suspicion
of his sanity. After a year

he added a deck on the starboard side, put in a Jacuzzi
big enough for himself, his wife, kids,
and that couple from Hendersonville polite enough
to buy one of his rowboats.

Another year, another deck, and he had fifty feet
square lumbering around his mast.
He sold the animals, sprayed
with Roundup, and the green

sea there since the Depression
dried up. The snakes
found somewhere else
to be handled.

Finally, he enclosed the whole
with a rainbow of rafters, then shingled
them over with red oak, no longer a nut
but a neighbor.

Now he waits at the tiller, sunk
in his living room, next to the VCR, praying
God doesn't wash away the world
he's befriended in good faith.

Fearful Symmetry

"It's time to bring all cats indoors and keep them there."
—John Balzar, *"Too Many Cats,"* Los Angeles Times

I won't even keen for my furniture.
The reupholsterers can cover for me.
But there'd be the rodential problem, moles, voles
turning American lawns into acres of individual
slices of green Swiss. Though
the snakes would take care
of it, eventually, restoring our Edens
to their original good
and mediocre.
Regrettably, then, there'd be
the serpentine problem, copperheads
knotted under the throats of our outdoor
spigots, like designer neckties—until
the teleherpetologists took
over, culling the most venomous
who'd knowingly refuse to bite the tongues
            of the glossolaliacants
and die. Then, of course, we'd have
that problem, but Christ
would take care of it, leaving
his little lambkin at home, safely outside.

Lunch at the Park

She could be at McDonald's, grazing. Odd.
But the unicyclist is praising God.

Both arms straight up, surrendered to September,
this blissful woman is amazing! God!

A six-year-old squirts her with his Mac-10.
The unicyclist still is praising God.

She wobbles patterns in the parking lot,
her Alphas and Omegas tracing God.

No Manichean bicycle, no trike
for her! Just One True Wheel, begracing God.

With her free hands, she balances all praise,
blessing three Clemson fans abasing God.

They snicker, shout "Raise *your* hands if you're Sure!
Hey, honey! Who you think you're racing? God?"

Her Walkman isn't tuned to their Big Game.
No touchdowns fill her ears, dispraising God.

In self-defense, she turns her volume up.
She's listening to a CD raising God.

And here's her extra point, which no one hears
but me: *I've turned my other cheeks—amazing God!*

PAUL ALLEN

The Drive Home After the Hearing

Back when one road led to another,
clover-leafed to this or that place
matched on a map on our long road trips,
however lost or turned around we were,
each road had another road to end on,
the last one always getting us home.
But dead-ends go on forever:
There's the pile of slag, pile of limbs,
woods, field, town, towns, state, states....

How do the cloistered mystics have it?
Desire to leave this world is a sign of progress
in this world? The ache in the absence of Christ
thrills them as proof He is there?
Well, let's see: According to that, Old Girl,
what with this world of settled differences
between us, we must be madly in love.

Remember the Blue Ridge trip?
We stopped for the girls and maybe a peacock
throw rug for Nancy and Albert—
a joke about the folk who sell that sort of thing.
Seemed funny at the time, no money at the time,
but a little bit of space left on the card.
Fellow running the store, which was strewn
along the highway half a mile,
said they'd just had "a incident": *Man fell*
out of his car, rolled down the hill into the creek.
Bled from the head. The current kinda sucked
his blood, but the cold slowed the whole thing down,

kept him alive a long time looking up.
Remember his breath when he came in close?
Now what you people make of that?
Ain't just that. The car went yonder on alone .
Would you think a car could take two curves all by itself?
Chance. Chance and slant of road kept it going.

Well, what do you think, my friend,
flame, co-signer?
Maybe in all this interminable
blink of an eye that has been our lives,
the closer we got to whatever we wanted back then—
the forever we wanted back then—
the farther away it seemed.
So like a couple of discalced Carmelites,
padding around in the morning
until every breakfast is brunch,
maybe we've come to grips
with the gripes of love:
So many nights back to back!
All that current and cold business,
and the man stuck in our minds
as we wound out of that state all night,
his dying all that time in the water:
Remember how glad we were it wasn't us back there?
How you said it and I said it—glad it wasn't us
in the mountain's cold creek.
Do you think we're beginning to know now
that maybe—scary as it is—it was?

Ground Forces in the Academy

Some of us—older, more benign—
Always thought there ought to be a sign
For war: some demarcation where
Battles have names, maps are marked with stars,
Where officers and smooth politicos
Tap their pointers to show us how it goes.

Our era, though, brings vagueness: War on Terror?
Where is that? Terror is no Trafalgar,
Sebastopol, Bannockburn, Bull Run.
Where to send the arrow, aim the gun?
And when it's done, where will emplacements
Lie, covered in tender grass, and monuments
With grandchildren reading names, almost moved?
War is not war on terror.
                                        Only love
Is. The young know this; they've always known
The terror of a soul gone dead, fly-blown.
Their innocence forces them to see
Everywhere lost love's casualties.
They know them in some child-like way of knowing
They can't explain.
                              And so they may, in spring,
Say, walk the Appalachian Trail with friends
Against the terror that maybe this spring ends
All springs. Or loving, stroll dangerous streets.
Or believe in the face of obvious deceits.
Half-grown, grown, they come with groaning hearts
Set on some great battle in the arts
Of learning. They straggle in from city, farm,
Knowing what ancients knew: Four loves inform
All computations, facts, philosophy—
Affection, Eros, friendship, charity.

They know Descartes to be irrelevant,
As is distinguishing poem from elephant,
Or how to solve for x, or parse a verb,
Or tell an ancient poison from an herb.
Learning such is merely mimicry
Unless they gain a greater victory,
Which is to die, and dying be reborn
In wisdom where they come to know the thorn
And rose as identical twins of the one grace.
War on terror? That war has no place
Except the hemispheres of heart and mind
(*Soul*, we like to call them when aligned).
For *soul*, read *soldier* under our command.
We arm our raw recruits as best we can.

He Loses Focus in His Lecture on "A Good Man Is Hard to Find"

It's about your position. First, the grandmother stands over the man-of-the
      house, rattling the gun of the day's news at his head. Then she sits
      in the car, then the diner—coming down to earth.
Finally, after her family has been killed elsewhere (sitting or standing, we do
      not know), she's as down to earth as she can be—below the earth,
      in a ditch.
And the Misfit shoots her when she gets confused and calls on Jesus, calls
      the Misfit Jesus, perhaps.
Now in your physics class you learned that two things cannot occupy the
      same space at the same time.
But that's in physics class. In the real world, they can. Goddamn, I've lived
      that way all my life—both: the one with the gun, murder on his
      mind, and the one in the ditch, a prayer of love and pity for him
      draining from her lips. . . And, and. . . .
      I'm so sorry. Dismissed.

KEN AUTREY

School Lunchroom, 1955

We filed in by class, handed sweaty quarters
to the girl tending the gray metal coin box.
In this domain of onion and candied yam,
we took what the hair-netted women ladled
onto our plates behind the steamy glass.
Always there were rolls, toasted and painted
lavishly with government surplus butter,
delicacy for which the word "sopping" was invented.

Late spring days, crowded at folding tables,
we plotted food fights, ten-year-old fingers itching
for greasy skirmish, a spoon of English peas catapulting
into the fifth grade section that would trigger all-out war:
gobs of mashed potato, clouds of mustard,
spurts of ketchup smearing the noon air.

We would eat only the golden rolls,
saving gravied Salisbury steaks and little wheels
of sliced tomato to sail across the lunchroom.
We would lob cartons of chocolate milk
like grenades, their spouts snapped open
to spew sweet arcs as they spun.

Even the principal, called when hostilities
broke out, would be powerless to restore order
in the face of such carnage. For this,
we would bear hunger into the afternoon.

But when Mrs. Mullins silently rose
from the teachers' table and walked her tray
to the conveyer belt, we followed
with our impeccable plates
and lined up alphabetically at the door,
a memory of butter glazing our lips.

Before the Wedding

My daughter sits
in a silk robe beside
the bedroom window.

Her hair is impeccable,
fixed in a bun the veil
will soon cover.

She is passive,
hands at rest
on her crossed legs.

She says little
as the attendants
move around her

like courtesans,
powdering her face,
preparing her dress.

For long moments
she stares out the window.
The Saturday sky is overcast.

A slight wind troubles
the late spring leaves.
She waits until the last

possible minute to rise
and begin to dress.
At the flourishing

of crinoline and lace,
I leave the room,
closing the door

on a covey of women
sipping champagne.
As I walk downstairs

their voices blur
like the murmur
of nesting birds at dusk.

Still Life with Piranhas

Billy O'Shea arced his hot dog
into the tank, and six of us watched
a flurry of fish become all teeth.
The knot untied as fast as it drew in,
and one pink shard of flesh remained
in the updraft. A silver flash,
and even that was gone.
                                    We knew
how scrawny Brazilian cows blunder
into a cool river, linger a moment
too long to evaporate into a cloud
of flashing scales. Five minutes, then nothing
but bones. That mustard-soaked wiener
was closer to home and not much bigger,
really, than some kid's finger.
When the class gathered at the snow cone stand,
the teacher must have wondered why we slurped
so slowly.
                        And later, when nobody
banged on the gila monster's glass
or rattled the monkey cages,
she figured the sun had sapped us.
That was several years ago. I can't recall
the teacher's name, and God knows how many
overheated cows have since been stripped
clean in the Amazon.
                                    Here I am lounging
in a wicker chair, engulfed by Sunday papers,
fingers smudged with news. They've arrested
a woman, 72, who neglected 112 Chihuahuas
in her home. She seemed confused.
No statement yet from the SPCA.
My one good suit collects dust
in the closet, and the wing-tips

go unpolished as I sort the facts.
This time I drop all pretense
of making them fit. I'm running
on faith.
                    You could say it's my religion,
this communion of piranha and Chihuahua,
zoo and sunny den, finger and hot dog.
What should matter: whether the cops let her
change the threadbare robe or handcuffed her
in the squad car. And the question
of whom she called from the station.
What I remember: how the water's surface
never broke, the snow cone froze me to the bone,
and cherry syrup pooled in my flimsy cup.

JAN BAILEY

Bloodroot

Bloodroot and bayberry, violets like buttons
popped willy-nilly in the woods. Ruby reds
and cherries delicate as spilled lace, the lilacs
close to fainting. In the yard, the oaks barely
breathe, so laden with vine, thick as a man's
thigh, but a scent so surely woman it aches
to lie beneath them; the finches almost frantic;

the silly, coupling squirrels; the bees, those flagrant
suitors, drunk as sailors. Our neighbor's Siamese
howls in her despair, dogs bay at anything that moves
and you, asleep on the sweet grass, tiny seeds
of sweat above your mouth, which dreams wide open.
Your hands burn. Let them wake.
Nothing they desire here will resist them.

Breath

Holding my breath for as long
as I was able, twelve years old
and in love with life—the very
yoke and seed of it—full blown
July, the foothills purple-faced,
waves of hay popping with cicadas
and nothing to do but luxuriate,
so I would practice holding my breath,
edging up on death, daring wisdom,
a kind of playful foreplay, pushing
to the very tip of pleasure just to shield
it, as those boys you read about who
hang themselves accidentally as they
masturbate, so ridiculous really,
this groove between ecstasy and ruin,
as if one could not exist without
the other, as if without the death
of anything, the pleasure's commonplace.

With What Wild Hand

Out from the crevices of the rocks
amid soda cans and Styrofoam, he

skimmed the shimmer of the pond
and toward the waterfall, a flapping

silver fish clamped in his tight snake's jaws.
It had just begun to rain and it seemed

the willows fanned further out, away
from the canopy of oaks. I stood

transfixed as he glided with such grace,
his head regal, intent, a boasting head,

the fish quiet now, and I the gaping
audience, though I doubt he knew it.

All day I felt the spectator and slowed
my pacing and watched the world lean

toward love. Desire and devour.
In the quick of an eye the toad unleashes

its tongue, a cricket stills. We know
the story—gristle to bear, and in the muscled

sinew of lion, the sleek flank of gazelle.
Just now I licked the salt from your lip,

your brow and swallowed your salt kiss.
It is dark, shadows are eaten—no blouse

across the chair, no stockings, no floor. To where
am I pulled, into what pool, with what wild hand?

FRAN BARRETT

Treasure

Field of grain ruffled
by sky's big hand. Feeling
calm. Feeling empty.
The yellow jeeps waving hello,
mocking with its vastness.

*

Two girls bury a friendship
box under the big oak,
vowing friendship forever.

"We are alone in the world," says one.

Far across the meadow, trees are emerald
fans dotted with diamonds.

"We're rich!" says the other.

A closer look? It's just *boys*
sitting high in the branches eating apples.

"Sometimes I want to coil myself around my mother's leg
and cling on like the vine I used to be but. . ."

The trees shimmer
as the boys shimmy
down brown trunks
called in for supper.

". . . I'm a big girl now."

*

They fix peanut-butter sandwiches and watch power
lines making smooth boundaries and contrast.
Draping the yellow horizon.

Lying side-by-side-by-side
the sun, the two friends.

Counting stars prophesied
nature collapsing. Stars are holes
in black felt, poked
through with a staple gun.

One friend has to move
every four years. (Step-dad
and coast-guard.)

Looming about the girls
at twilight's first nip. . .
the summer after sixth grade.

The sun is nowhere now.
Shooting moons drag across
black fabric, gashing it
like teardrops
not spoken for.

FREDERICK BASSETT

Women Who Plow

I'd heard Dad's stories about Mrs. Moore—
how her husband left for other dreams,
how she plowed an ox named Dan
until the land wore them out.

I knocked, expecting a bitter recluse
who dipped wormwood for snuff.
A hesitant face answered in a bonnet
and coarse dress that swished the floor.

"Dad sent me to cut you some wood."
"Then you must be Leon's boy."
Her soft voice led me to a dark kitchen
where I choked down a dried-apple pie.

In the barn, the red ox rose
from the dry dung through my nostrils.
The cracked wooden yoke hung
from a rusty hook on the wall.

I tried to imagine her striding
the furrows all day, hard as a man,
her one resolution even more adamant—
to die before asking for help.

Back then, I loved the way
Mrs. Moore could make a boy
feel like a grown man—
such praise for small favors.

These days, I love the way
she comes hobbling on the scene
from the shadows of my mind,
when I meet a hard plow woman.

Goat Rock

Down in Gadston Creek, some father
thing narrating the pilgrimage
as though one could take sons
to a time and place as strange
to them as the land of Goshen,
I named the tracks on the banks,
and they picked up the game,
guessing . . . arguing . . . pleasing me.
Dad, squirrel tracks, aren't they?
No, those are mink, like in mink coats.
The winter of '49, I ran a trap line
on this creek . . . steel traps, mind you.
Trapped a glossy mink just below here . . .
had to drown it with a stick.
They hold that last breath forever,
lungs heaving it back and forth.
Then, it rises bubble by bubble.
We sloshed on down the Gadston,
sliding over flat slippery rocks
that stretched across the course,
one after another, like descending stairs,
the banks rising thirty feet.
Above the old milldam, long broken,
ancient waters had sculpted Goat Rock
for a boy who would sit beneath the dome,
cloaked in legends of Creek warriors
and their last stand at Horseshoe Bend.
Silent as the sun, we sat that noon,
golden in our separate worlds.

Rock Springs Churchyard

I've been a long time coming, Maw Owen,
as if my whole life were one big detour.
I stopped on the way at your home place—
the barns all sagging, the house slumping
like a woman who has outlived ten children.
I tried to imagine that early April scene
when you rode home in the buggy,
embracing for the first time a slender girl
from Taylor's Crossroads, who, at twelve,
had watched her mother and father rattle
that last breath and settle back for the grave.
I've heard the story in Mother's own words.
How you tried to calm her fears
with promises of a bright new dress.
How Gertrude asked, "What shall she call you?"
"Maw," you said, never pausing the rocker.
Once, as I studied those old photos,
Jeanette said that Mother was more like you
than any of your own children.
Would that I could have said it myself.
Would that I knew the sound of your voice.
Oh, there was time. Time and then time.
But here I stand amid the marble ears
of these tombstones overlooking
Corn House Creek, a stranger,
with nothing but a mouthful of words.

MICHAEL BASSETT

Something About the Way She Touches

I'm watching the way she coaxes
him into hitting her again.
It is an intimate thing, weirdly
ritualistic, like my mother burying
a burnt turkey in the snow.
Something about the way she touches
the tip of her tongue to her bloody lip,
about the way his hand, red and hovering
somewhere between striking and reaching out,
reminds me of being a boy
in the backyard at twilight, waiting
for the wind to make something beautiful
from the tears of pear trees.

Awakenings

A woman sticking her finger into an aquarium
watches it turn into a goldfish. Her
plunging fist scuttles off
as a blue crab; her arm up to the elbow,
an electric eel.

She is a mermaid, deathless blue
back-floating, old tiara
and string of pearls.

She thinks about the bathtub
with its cracks and stains.
Thinks about the sound
of running water, her husband's voice.

She saunters up the stairs. But the tub
has burst through the plaster
and waddles down Main
on iron feet, chasing
a wet dream all its own.

Slugs

Sometimes when I sit on a bench
and watch people strolling by, I think
this one will die of congestive
heart failure, that one will blacken
in a mattress fire, this young mother
will end tripping on a toy ninja, that cop
choking on a peppermint stick.

When I was eleven, neighborhood boys
and I would gather slugs from our mothers'
gardens. They were vaguely beautiful
like the inside of clam shells, sunlight
in gasoline, a cobalt and ash flake sky
reflected in water. We'd meet
at the lake with our mason jars and float out
a wriggling pile on a piece of plywood.

Before long, the birds would come.
We'd stare at the diving beaks
picking slugs off one by one. Some,
dislodged by the commotion, fell—
or, as we liked to think, drowned
themselves, desperate with horror.

Rachel Smoke was the most voluptuous
of the three Smoke sisters.
After we had scraped up the $20,
she sprinkled salt in her mouth,
cupped a fat slug in her palm,
then slowly drug it across
the edge of her bright pink tongue.
Now that would be, we
moaned, the way to go.

CLAIRE BATEMAN

Distinction

CONGRATULATIONS!

You (*insert name here*) have just won a UNIQUE & FABULOUS
    PRIZE.

Within the next 24 hours, you are GUARANTEED to receive the
    one & only COMB OF THE WORLD—authentic, conveniently
    pocket-sized, the distance between individual teeth measurable
    only by Scanning Electron Microscope (complimentary cathode-
    ray vacuum tube & fluorescent screen included).

Yes! With THE original fine-tooth comb, you can finally bid
    farewell forever to these armies of predatory dust mites
    rampaging through your carpet; the pseudomonades clinging to
    your dishtowel; the fungi burrowing through your plaster walls.

And by simply combing the air around you, you can obtain
    ongoing relief from bronchial congestion & ocular irritation
    due to such unseen atmospheric impurities as volcanic ash;
    pulverized bone, hair, & skin; magnetized iron filings; residue
    of feathers & spider eggs; all varieties of catalytic powders;
    ammoniac, sulfuric, & phosphorescent gases; chimney soot;
    fish scales; anthrax powder; floating ink & gold dust.

Romance, finances, or career in knots? THE COMB OF THE
    WORLD's ever-efficient micro-filtrating action is guaranteed
    to loosen & release the physically constricting clove hitch,
    timber hitch, bowline, & slipknot, as well as all varieties of
    syntactical and epistemological entanglings, irrelevancies,
    obfuscations, & infelicities.

No more shadowy rustlings in the soul's undergrowth. No more
   tough little colonies of unregenerate sadnesses, or ragged
   ambiguities scuttling just out of reach. And those nearly
   imperceptible holes migrating through the rippling fabric
   of your etheric body?—you can comb them all out even as
   they rise!
And last but not least, though we possess only ABSOLUTE
   CONFIDENCE in our product, for your additional security
   & piece of mind, THE TWEEZERS OF THE WORLD will be
   included for free.

How We Fall

Nobody does a swan dive
into Jesus.
Instead, we fall
bleeding or weeping;
we fall clawing the air
as if to climb it
all the way back;
we fall shrieking, unraveling,
all angles and knobby joints,
all stutter & sputter,
our teeth rattling,
our hair fanning out like flames;
we fall foaming at the mouth
with hypothesis & self-argument;
we fall mutely,
hoarding our breath
as if breath withheld
could possibly
make a difference.
And it's as if the falling
has a mind of its own,
episodic, all fits & starts,
overlapping time zones & air pockets,
so that sometimes a faller seems to arrive
just prior to departure,
& other times a faller seems to be merely
hovering in mid-air
like Bugs Bunny,
unaware that he's left
the edge of the cliff behind.
Some of us even fall
from the inside out
or the outside in,
the soul preceding the body

or the body the soul
the trajectories describing
all sorts of arcs & parabolas,
disregarding every rule of descent,
demolishing every point of etiquette.

Reprieve

The same day the doctor confirmed my mother's pregnancy, he also informed her that she was carrying not one but two children—twins, one human female, the other a pearl. "They are chemically incompatible," he said. "You must choose in favor of one, who will then absorb the other, or you will surely lose them both." Cruel dilemma for a woman who not only possessed a strong maternal instinct, but loved the beautiful and mysterious as well! For the proverbial three days and three nights she pondered, unable to make up her mind. Finally, however, as if to register my own opinion, I gave a feeble kick, a gossamer flutter, and that decided her, so dutifully, though with considerable sorrow, she began an intense course of balancing the medicine the doctor gave her, and my sister the pearl gradually weakened, finally dissolving into me. Had she been the one with fishy little legs and arms—in other words, had *she* been human and *I* a pearl—no doubt she'd have done the same thing, and I wouldn't have begrudged her this feeble gesture toward self-preservation, so I'm certain she experienced no rancor as she felt herself begin to come apart.

Surely there are many aspects of my nature that can be explained only by her presence in my bloodstream—for instance, my acute sensitivity to sunlight; any true pearl would sell the very soul she doesn't have for five minutes of shade. There's nothing a pearl detests more than daylight—in fact, she goes into a kind of hysterical coma in sunshine, recovering from her swoon only in the safety of her long, black-velvet-lined box. I myself get migraines from glare, burn easily, and would, if permitted, permanently hibernate indoors. That's why all year round I wear enormous black sunglasses the ridicule of passersby. Also, like a pearl, I am mostly a loner, and I tend to surround myself with loners, just as each pearl pierced through by the same golden chain basks in the luminescence of the others even as she secretly believes she's the only one suspended there, and wines, "I'm so lonely."

As for differences between my sister and me—were you surprised when I mentioned that a pearl has no soul? It's true; you can test this for yourself: candle her like an egg, and all you'll find is a cool cloudiness; send

X-rays through her with the most state-of-the-art lauegram, and all you'll see is that tell-tale hexagonal pattern of dots designing the crystalline structure; slice her in half and all you'll discover is layer upon layer of aragonite—no true core at the center, only the original parasite or grain of sand, not a soul but an anomaly, an intrusion, though come to think of it, a human soul does feel to its bearer, that is, to me, not unlike an irritation, so maybe in this aspect too, we are more alike than different.

Very probably, then, I'm a pearl on the inside and a human on the outside, in which case my mother is *not*, as she assumed all these years, guilty of my sister's death, for in choosing me she saved both of us, and thus, she can unshackle herself from the underwater rock where she has been doing penance all these years, her chin barely above the surface.

LIBBY BERNARDIN

Spirit

And the great white pelicans
lifted themselves with such
grace that I felt some blessing fall upon us
from the black-tipped wings gathering air,
pulling themselves away from earth
as though a white shawl had shook itself,
then folding back in the wind, took our breath
from us with long orange-yellow beaks,
then circled back, on Marsh Island
on ocean shore, sand, grass,
mystical feet gathered into some
300 count of white plumage—
magnificent restless stalking,
we unwilling to leave what we were given
so that turning away, our hearts stirred
by the true splendor of a thing,
I stared longingly over our wake,
nothing illusory in the parting white foam,
nothing unreal in the beating wings.

When you find love

Seize it; not in a lustful way, but as though
you have stumbled upon something remarkable,
say a winter wren, fledgling grounded under
dense brush almost hidden in morning's waking
a horse nearby, his nose burrowed in snow

Cup it as though consecrated,
Place it in the nest from which
It has taken to the air:
     Do not ask it to meet your needs
     Do not ask it to choose
     Do not ask anything of it

Think instead of how it might be when
finally there is the feel of feet on limb
little wings ballooning out
trusting as it plunges until it can soar—

Grateful for gentle hands
that set it in sheer joy of journey,
grateful for shadows of crisp cedars
pointing toward season's unspoken Word.

New Moon Going Down in the Western Sky

for Phil

Tonight I came upon the moon so low
I could have plucked her from the Western sky
A rose, a shimmer of dew as Planets pin
across the sky—Mars, Venus, Jupiter, Saturn—one
of them at the soft curved edge of that smiling mouth.

That's the way she is, capricious, ambiguous,
a message I am unable to ravel, yet there
before me, real and honest the way my heart
feels when I am with you. Why am I given
this sight that blinds, yet helps me to know

I am just a woman who could love a man
who knows the moon, has green eyes,
a bear's heart, fierce in strength and gentleness,
who lives under the water sign,
who I once knew in a long ago dream
when we sat in a canoe in the marsh
marveling at the moon about to give rain,
about to explain the way we were to be
though we couldn't have understood.

This moon tonight, the farmers say, is holding water,
refusing her rain. Still, water lilies grow along a road
a Zambian basket holds rose petals and shore found rocks
I sift through bramble of grief, toward shimmer,
I can come in now I say to her, gathering
her teardrop petals, gathering you.

LAUREL BLOSSOM

Morbid Fascination

If as a boy you lived in a land of women
Languid but for the first flushed moments
Following the latest letter from the Front;

Or, like me: when asked to watch my little sister,
I watched the sled come hurtling toward her
Down the white hill of my fascinated heart;

Maybe, in the aftermath of the execution,
We all feel the urge to work our fingers in
The holes of his body the condemned man loved.

On the ocean floor, where earth's core
Erupts and water does not boil,
Huge sulphur-breathing tube worms, eels, clams

The size of dinner platters,
Red-blooded crabs and mussels dwell,
Who do not need the sun or grace or oxygen at all.

The Papers Said

In Kenya they have two paved highways.
Commuters throw garbage out the windows to baboons
so used to being fed this way
they wait at intervals like pets or trashcans.
One day a man threw out an orange
he'd filled with chili powder just for the hell of it

to see what would happen (it
rolled in the red dust at the highway's
edge) because the man hated those fucking baboons
or whatever the word is in Swahili, the way
they jerk off at the side of the road, or show their
            disgusting red cans
to each other, and this one not especially orange

orange
got picked up by one of those fuckers, who pushed it
into his mouth and bit down. The white man in the green car
            on the liquid red highway
under the burning blue sky (or whatever the baboon
word is for hellfire)—the man in the green car went
            his way.
Baboons scream as only baboons can.

The man felt merciful; no more living trashcans.
He forgave his wife. As the sky turned the brilliant orange
of an African sunset, he drove home. It
gratified him to see the sides of the highway
deserted, the entire baboon
population he'd driven away.

For a while, he went out of his way
to be nice to his wife and children. He let them
            watch American

T.V.; on the weekend he bought a six-pack of orange
pop, packed it
in the car and took them all for a drive along the highway.
Of course the baboons

were back; he expected that. *Baboon*
Attacks, however, he did not expect, especially the way
it seemed to recognize the green car (uncanny,
the papers called it), hurled itself at the open window
        when an orange
shape glistened briefly there, and ripped the man's throat
        out. Call it
whatever you like, poetic justice, but people aren't safe
        on the nation's highways,

the papers said.

How I Can Tell

I was looking down at the ground
the front wheel zigzagged and the seat beneath me wobbled
the house was burning down
I walked across the street by myself inside myself

I looked both ways I looked up I woke up
my father picked me up in his arms what's the matter
don't ever I've been looking for you the sky
turned black at noon I fell off I got up the house is on fire

to your room I was lost I thought you were dead
he carried me down the stairs he was crying
I looked up the wheel was going straight I went
to my room and stayed there I could feel

the line through my spine
it was right it was going to be all right
we watched the house
once you've got it inside you you always

CATHY SMITH BOWERS

Shadow Dancing

I wish Miss Saylo could've seen
the night my brother said, *Go Limp*,
then swirled me in his arms across

the discotheque, light and lithe,
more graceful than I had ever been,
she who'd put an end to my dancing

days. She was tiny and all pruned up,
like those photos I never understood
of vegetables dressed like people,

ribbed peppers sporting glasses,
tomatoes in tutus and tiaras. She
carried a big stick, nudged to attention

our clavicles and ribs if we slouched
in our pliés or rendered too soft
our arabesques. I tried to do what she

instructed. Pretended to be that leaf
fluttering from its tree, oh, down
and twirling down I went, landing

in a tangled mass amidst the fine
and tutored elegance of the other girls.
When she shouted, *Stop!* it took a moment

to realize she was talking to me,
though grace of some sudden other
kind made her wait until later

to relegate me to the stool
by the record player
where until semester's end

I would raise and lower the needle
at her command. So it was she
I thought of years later,

in the unschooled pedagogy
of my brother's arms, beautiful
in his white suit, the pink shirt

with pearl buttons he would keep
for years, long after the disease
had ravaged him, the Bus Stop

and the Hustle having entered, too,
oblivion's faithful realm. *Go
limp*, was all he said, and I did,

each lift and trill of the Bee Gees'
bright falsettos waking the long
muted language of my body.

Even Andy was not dead yet.

First Year Teacher

During an impassioned lecture
on the three principal parts
of *hang* and *hang*,
I turned from my grainy
etchings across the board
and in the voice
of a would-be pundit
whose moment had finally come,
said, "Please remember, class,
men cannot be hung."

The laughter began
a ripple down the aisle,
a prurient note
passed from desk to desk
until the entire class
let loose a roar.

When they finally gained composure,
someone said,
"Couldn't it just be
you've had bad luck
with men?"

The Living Daylights

She'd beat it out of all
of us, she warned, if we
dared defy her rules,

tried her thinning patience
one more time. Truth is, she
never laid a hand on anyone,

though once, for some small
forgotten truancy, she snatched
me without warning from my play,

swatting at my behind
with a belt she'd grabbed
from its too-convenient hook

on the closet door, and oh
what a sight together there
we made, round and round

the living room, a windmill,
top, fine whirligig, bright wheel
and she the axis to my screeching

spoke. By the time she finally
ceded me the win, not a lick
had grazed the small but quicker

shins that carried me bruise-free
into womanhood, I who fared
no worse than the neighbor kids

who bore into the world deep marks
of defter hands. She's gone
now, benign and hopeless queen

of discipline, the daylights
beaten, in the end,
out of all of us.

FARLEY BRIGGS

Gray Monkey

There's a gray monkey on the patio.
He has a bowl of anemones.
My husband is appalled when
he spots him so near the green
resin furniture with the matching
umbrella and the potted caladium leaves
and the baskets of trailing ivy.
He says he'll ruin it all; says he'll
get rid of him. The monkey holds his ground.
He's a sudden whim set in concrete—
and he'll stay right where he is—
bringing me flowers.

Opening

The lifted cover
frees a breath of age,
of crumbling paper, yellowed
library paste,
the closed-in smell of long neglect.
The scraps of early lives
crowd to the corners.
Faded newsprint echoes
wedding plans, a garden party—
long departed guests.
A brittle stem is pinned
to a valentine, the darkened rose
as thin as the lacy heart.
Unmarked by time's abusive hand,
smooth, eager faces, bold
in black and white, look toward
the camera: my mother plays
in rare Southern snow;
my father laughs, waves
from a beach; their brothers, sisters—
even the smallest dead.
Here they're bound together,
gladly young—before we joined
in their futures and my past.

STEPHEN COREY

The Blooming of Sentimentality

I hear it coming from the start,
the claptrap all shamelessly marshaled:
the hordes of muted violins
swelling and subsiding, the voice
wrenching to a wail I know
makes a cheap-shot bit for my heart.

I keep it all at a distance,
looking askance at the hangdog eyes
or the child's squeal and her sparkling smile—
these images that must not count
because they are designed to count,
to demand the shiver of my skin
for the whimper of a half-pound pup.

Time after time I fend it off,
the chorus of grandmothers, roses, and tears.
It seems to fall from the sky,
to sprout from the ground by night—
rootless, and puffed with hope.
I focus instead on integrity:
wholeness and balance of mood,
visions that come from those depths
where freshness and honesty breed,
where clans of thin motives and still-thinner words
lack the power and desire to go.

But on one dark, soulful day
these violins rise up again,
so many I picture a wave,
the sweeping bows like grain
rippling to the far horizon.
And through that deafening swell,
my lovers and family march uphill
to a flowered ridge glued on a crystal sky,
where the Enemies cannot reach them.
This *could* be the place, I suddenly think,
and I run to reach that distant height,
my arms outstretched and raised
in that gesture of exaltation

I have always seen but never known.
And then, I am beside myself as well,
cheering me on as I run.

I reach the sun-drenched edge and I know
I have cut off the dullness of reason
to set loose a burgeoning dream
that could give all my other dreams range.

Past, Present, Future

Like the burn of sex we want it again—
that moment from the past we thought we had
but lost, jolted, as we lose at waking

the wisp that led to nightmare's tears or screaming.
That day, or hour, seemed a rock in the hand.
Like burn of sex we want it, again

and again, our whole lives' narrow-track bodies
never bored by lust, by memories' clutch—
those sun-hot monuments to *have* turned *had*.

Miles-long view from hill, taste of milk or rain,
wind-cut face, parents alive without pain—
these we covet, like the burn of sex, again . . .

Dear Reader, this is not what you think,
not bedroom talk, nor family-album time
flipping through stacked moments we'd wish ahead.

No, this is the passing world, which had a history
until we turned against the future,
bludgeoned both—*was* and *might be*—with the present:
Stunned moments and thoughts. Burned-out sex. Had. Have not. Won't.

The Ugly Stepsisters

We hobble blind through the world—alive.
What would you do to be touched by the prince?
Toss your own toes under the bed
before he entered, sit with your back turned coyly
to slide your bloody foot into the slipper?
What would you give for that ride beside him?
The parading moment with the castle in sight
before those pigeons cried you down:
"Look, the right bride sits at home!"
Even after the thing you loved was given,
once more, to the beautiful, would you limp and crawl
to the church, dreaming of one more chance?
When those damned pigeons gouged your eye
but left you with one to watch the wedding,
when you knew they would be waiting after in the trees,
would you leave the church to walk home, knowing
you were right?
                    Beauty loses nothing when it pays court
to ugliness. We cried when we saw how she fixed our hair—
what could we do but ask for more?
In some far corner of the earth, beside her skin
old blood stains the deepest recess of the slipper.
We feel it still, that moment when we made it fit.

ROBERT CUMMING

The Way West

Watching the world unfold itself
now, December, in the garden,
collards bushing up
under grey snow clouds,
barley sprouts in the field,
green haze over red clay,
two deer in the fringe pines
ears up, ready to run,
mistletoe clenched to the high oak
darker than squirrels' nests,
white smoke from the stacks in town,
other fields, woods beyond,
on west to the mountains,
I think this is the way
unfolding like a field,
no terror, no congratulations,
eat and stretch when we want to,
listen, watch,
clench or run when we need to,
for your life, my life.

Seagoing

We gave the bed fifteen hours
drowsing, waking, drowsing again.
It gave us eons, and seas,
scorch times, ice times, neap tides and flood tides,
drawing us up by the flare of the nightlight—
into the bathroom, stretch—
but down again, quick, in the undertow dark
with our whispers, *Let me tell you
your ageless dream that you don't know you're dreaming.
No, me, let me tell you yours!*
Your hands flowing around and under me
ringing my body like a buoy's bell.

PHEBE DAVIDSON

Staying Cool

She is sitting on her screened porch on an August night. She can hear them. The yips and yodels fade and get louder, fade and get louder. Her dress is pale green and where its scooped neck lifts a little from her collarbone the skin glistens with the delicate skim of sweat that she always wears on summer nights. She sips from a glass of gin and tonic then holds the glass against her cheek for the coolness. She has lost one barn cat and old dog so far. She sits here evenings to listen. Sometimes she turns on the flood lights and watches the yard. She likes things to be consistent. She always has her gin and her delicate skim of sweat.

Broad Daylight

He liked motorcycles. He liked beer. He liked this one woman lived up in North Carolina. He liked to drive fast on hot nights and throw his empties over the roof his car. One time he went into the wood. He said he was going in to shoot some squirrels. He might shoot some. He liked being in the woods. He kept moving and he looked at everything hard. He liked wearing his old canvas high tops and he set an easy pace. He'd been in the woods two, maybe two and half hours when it started to bother him. A little tic of motion he thought he saw from the outside corner of his left eye. And again. Every time he thought he saw it he'd lose it again and it would be just the woods, the way it always was. Shadow and green. Maybe something would start a bird, or something high up would shake a few leaves. Walking in second growth, he swung his head to his left without altering stride. Doggy muzzle. Pointed ears. Yellow eyes. Then it disappeared. He kept walking till he got to the road. All the way home he thought he was slicker than snake shit.

Up Long Cane

Old Coyote goes up by Long Cane Creek. Sun is shining. Sky is very blue. He sniffs and reads the wind. He finds some brush back from the road where he can lie up and see what there is. Cars coming off the highway ramp. A man and woman at the edge of the woods not doing anything. He sees a handful of hawks circling above the power lines. Three middle-sized kids poking around in a ditch. He curls himself up in a coyote ball. Puts his tail up over his nose. He takes a nap.

KWAME DAWES

Sketch

With graphite I soften your bones,
make exotic the absence of your lashes,
and your fingers, long and elegant,
cradle a plum, the light of its juice
flaming vermillion through the taut skin.

I etch out your gaze, tender, tender
about your forehead where the howl
of darting pain creases all, softly
as if, in the soft lead, I can calm
it all, make it go away. You are going.

With the soft of my palm's heel
I caress the bald glow of your head,
then clean a grey line where your brows
were—now there is nothing—
these markings of what you have suffered.

These days, bodies crumble
about me, the dead, desperate for healing
grow weary, stoic, then quietly go.

My blackened fingers make you round,
plumb as a fruit just plucked.
Tomorrow I lift you, bird of bones,
limbs softly collapsed.

There is sunlight crawling across the lawn.
Despite the drought, it's resiliently green,
except the narrow path of old sod we laid,
now traumatized by neglect into a crude buzz-cut;
and this, too, is a symbol of our loss.

It is August in Columbia. Nothing
can fight in this heat. Just stay
still, maybe a small wind will
blow, maybe a small wind.

The Glory Has Left the Temple

for Gabriel Garcia Marquez

To tell it, I could call it a dream.
A dream of the Caribbean coast of Colombia
where a beautiful black man serves
thick omelets, messy with onions and mushrooms
to an assortment of mavericks, dock workers,
professors, maids, three police officers,
five whores and a clutch of lawyers at midnight;
sopping up the curdling rum in their bellies
with thick chunks of white doughy bread.
Antonio, the black chef in flowing linen
has a hand jutting from his belly
to hold hot coals, and above his head
the interlocking whirling wheels
with shifting eyes blink back tears
and follow our every movement. The earth
has grown weary with too much blood.
Everyone is counting the casualties
like the score of soccer matches.
I could call it a dream, a kind of
Marquezian apocalypse, the memoir
of a novelist being handed the reams
of paper on which he will prophecy
to the wind. Instead, I will admit
the truth: I have been sitting in a hot
room smelling rich with incense
and the sweat of the priests who have lost
the language to comfort the bereaved;
priests whose idols have crumbled
to dust. I am listening to the wind,
to the voice in the wind telling me
to write it all down. So I do.

Brother Love

for Kojovi

It is familiar soil: the constancy of the hills
there each morning, the rituals of burying the dead,
the sound of names not heard for years on the radio,
the constant tragedy of their sudden passing,
the smell of food—oily, coconut sweet,
thick, wafting through the heat from the mango
tree darkened cluster of wood houses;
prayers as revealing as gossip in the congregation
of boredom. We are doing it all together. These things
are lost in exile and it *is* exile, this away-ness, this freedom
where we are fluttering in the wind with no reliable
anchor. My brother, we are strangers sometimes,
growing in our own locked worlds.
Then in a Kingston sunset, we knock fists
as you turn into the boyish grinner for an instant.
I discover again your brilliant eyes and we laugh
at the familiar code of silence, knowing, knowing
not to question it, but to hold on to the myth
of our history, the comfort of laughter,
the security of a desperately tight embrace—
knowing it is in these tidy instances that we find
we have grown together despite the miles and years.

KEN DENBERG

Baby, It's Cold Outside

As if it weren't enough, the whole world drunk
spinning out of orbit, my hair on end
hung over, the last ativan dissolves
in a glass of stale wine, forgetting you
for a second, my mind on the fizzing
the room does a worse turn, a boom, then down.

Telling your spiritual advisor you
won't ever do this again won't save your
sorry ass—c'mon now, lie down in this bed
of brambles, those pinpricks of regret might
stir some action. Right angles leaning wrong
everyone you don't like sees your movie
laughing, telling on you in perfect quotes—
something comes and goes, a breath in my hair.

Blueberry Pie

A perfect circle, a wolf star in your eye.
Birds are flying on her dress. The limit of all science

is what we know most about history. Goethe's tattered sweater.
In war days we rationed sugar, dark bread.

At night we lie down together like spoons, listen
to what we think is thunder.

What scares you most in this, this tiny universe?
I'd like another slice of pie.

No, I don't pray for anything anymore.
In winter the wind, the wind polishes ice,

the ice is the only thing between us drowning.
My neighbor builds a large boat. A drought for months.

I want to tell her she is my life, but nowadays
that coming from a man is weakness.

I've laid off the clubs for home. I've laid off
all sensation. I've butterflies in my head.

Bag your tools and let's ride, but first,
please, another piece of pie.

Kiss Me

It is raining the tears of a million sins
so we ask forgiveness, it will never
happen again and going on, thinner
purged, a bit purer or guiltless, remorse
a thing of the past no matter what we
did, but the gray rain, the tall white buildings
impersonal drifts of snow along the streets
the hellos or goodbyes, shutting the doors
or opening them to the cold shoulder
of the world, this cascade, this gentle wave
of a hand, it's nothing, doesn't matter
anxiety only momentary
and hopelessness of our desire
          that temporary thing we gently kiss.

CURTIS DERRICK

Reading Keats

Beauty has no antidote. Ingest its germs,
your heart is prone to be a sump,

swamped by the all-consuming love
of being all consumed. Thus, the term:

Romantic. As in the work of Keats, whose lungs,
hemorrhaging, still filled with grace—

damp hothouses, from which he coughed
bouquets of verse, and in whose hands,

each blossom turned to gem. Words
faceted and weighed.

We've heard their silences and light
kaleidoscope. One trope goes dark, another

brightens on the beat—breaths of color—
music our hearts can whistle with. Pumping

without sleep that swell welling-up of hue
we call desire, which eats a poet whole.

Diamond trill of twilight nightingale.
Sapphire autumn sky. Swallows

on hunger-hurried wings. The air,
alive with appetites. Heaven, we see here,

parting as we pass, closing in behind us
once we do. The invisible, so ambient,

even now it melts us in its mouth;
leaves us longing for yet another taste.

Rest Area

The raw-boned man with Clorox bucket
swabs tables down—trustie from the pen,
frail from cancer, fifty years of prison food.
"Queers," he spits. "Goddamn 'em!"
The Doppler whine of traffic down the slope.
Nights, it's true. Cast off from home, here
men merge, bold as hunching spaniels
on your lawn. They roll anonymous
on the grass, fold over tables, loll
in liquors of pure release
and leave via highway artery,
like the Johnsons just arrived
by Winnebago.
                    Two days down
out of Duluth, in route to a beach,
three kids disgorge, lope free, fan out, exploring.
Mom, towing toddler, moseys up the walk.
Dad, stretching legs with Rex on the leash,
bristles at the mutt's misbehavior
on a bare patch of ground.
                         The plot's scent
shakes Rex like a chamois. With shoulders,
he buffs the place hard. Groans
of erasure. Lead taut, Johnson yanks
at the shepherd. Rex yanks back.
The man who loves him, red-faced,
cursing, drags him off by the throat.

Kids, with the con, laughing
at the hullabaloo.

Red Johnson at the Crab Legs Bar

Wigwammed two weeks with his tribe of five
in the Winnebago, he's a regular now.
"What'll it be, Red?" "The usual."
And the usual, aside from scotch-on-the-rocks,
is eying up Cathy, Rose, and Beth. He decides
he loves them all and they all love him.
With easy grins, tanned limbs, southern drawls,
they've brightened up his stay and cashed him in.

But tonight's his last. And he's lost in the thought
of them with him in the Chieftain, rolling up
to the VFW back in Duluth. Him tanned too,
looking ten years younger. "One more, Rose.
For the road," he says. Once returned

to the truth at hand, Beth sidles up:
"Not so fast, Red. How 'bout a picture?
Cathy, get the SureShot." They squeeze in.
Halter tops and cut-offs. In a flash—
flashing legs and grins with arms intertwined,
they crown him. If not "King of the Road," surely
the VFW. Packed off with a Polaroid, pecks
on his cheek: "Y'all come back now, Red."

SKIP EISIMINGER

Recycling the Elements

"Then the dust shall return to the earth as it was,
and the spirit shall return unto God who gave it."
Ecclesiastes 12:12

The decompression of heart and brain
should let my soul make its sighing exit.
Assuming proper ventilation,
the gases will vanish up the flue
and the winds will divvy my flatulence.
Methane and phosphorus should flash blue-green
and head straight to some black hole starved for light.
Blood and sweat will gradually boil off
and join Aeolus filling the stomata
of Pickens County and the moons of Mars.
In minutes, only the solids will remain—
enough iron for a ten-penny nail—
some of the same stuff, I imagine,
that stiffened the spines of Jesus and Judas.
Though the skull may require a pestle,
please till the carbon and calcium
into that bed of perennials—
those carnations and sweet william
we weeded and fed for thirty years—
just a tick of the cosmic clock now.
Watch for me in the spring.
Should you choose to wear me upon your breast,
draw me, dear, into your lungs one last time.

On the Uncaused Cause

"Since it's now proven
that photons pop up spontaneously
in vacuums like the Virgin's womb,
nature had no creator
any more than Jesus did—
they just happened,"
the noted physicist noted.

"Since the universe was itself
once a photon,
there need not have been
a primordial battery or divine generator,"
he continued.

"And since photons emerge *ex nihilo*
and vanish *in nihilo,*
nature contains the seeds
of its birth, death, and perhaps rebirth.
Indeed, shit happens,"
he said, unmindful of the needles
in a skein of analogies.

But as Blake observed,
what is proven was once imagined.
And what isn't—like the moment before creation—
is answered in a thousand sermons and poems.
Someone always gets it right.
But the world is like the Internet—
open one site,
and a dozen thresholds beckon.

Thanks to Pasteur's wire screen,
we know the maggots in turds
are not spontaneous. And
as for combustion, someone
has to toss those oily rags in a pile.

The backs of our eyelids are screens—
some like those in a theater
are opaque;
others like Pasteur's
let the light through
and our vision out.

JAMES ENELOW

Manhattan Transfer

for Jim Peterson

Between Chinatown and Harlem
the bus is jolted to a stop,
and one seat up an Italian child
an her mother linger
over last night's crumpled playbill.
Outside, dealers position tables
for three-card monte scams.
Loudmouths pass flyers,
wholesale jewelry, bargain prices,
and everything's negotiable.
A crowd piles in,
snatching up most spots.
Then, she enters,
slowly moving along the aisle.
Silk skirt hugging tan legs.

The driver twirls one
of his dreadlocks and guns
the bus, jarring her
before she can find a seat.
She stumbles for a strap
to hang on to, I strain for her,
offering my seat.
Smiling, she sits and I catch the smell
of cinnamon and apples
as I whiff past her hair.
Our eyes attract slowly at first.
Our mouths do not move.

I look at her face, the small dimple
on the back of her neck,
the coiled strand of loose hair,
the tight fold of her ear
and my lips wet
wanting to kiss her, anywhere.
So we stare, stealing glimpses,
batting eyelids and blushing
while a Hispanic family up front
talks about making the rent.

By the next time the bus brakes
we're on our second date
and I'm sitting next to her
thanks to someone who left.
By the third halt we're married,
she's expecting in June
and I've already picked our
wallpaper and paint.
She shuffles in her seat
and I shift in mine,
we examine our views
about our child's future
and the school he'll attend.
We're in mutual agreement
without ever speaking.

After he's graduated
the bus snaps to her stop,
she signs divorce papers
and slips from the bus,
taking a transfer,
I am left
waiting for the next woman
to enter my life.
Outside,
a three-card monte dealer
snatches a young man's twenty.

Remembering Mayflies

That Easter, we felt our bodies
changing, somehow, beyond our means.
Once our parents turned away,
we slipped into the water
beneath the boarded walk,
and our bodies chilled in the shallow cold.
In that divided shadow, we thought
of snakes wrapping pillars
or spiders descending with venomed sin.

For years, we flinched from unseen fears
but only felt the sudden fin
brush our thighs and shoot away.
The uncertain rhythm of those waves
lapped along our shivering forms
and made us close the space between us.
Trembling, our lips hovered a breath away,
as the weeds wrapped our legs,
and we, in turn wrapped one another.

Above us, cocoons stretched in our heat
as the soft cotton moved
each moment we moved,
and we watched as a miracle changed along with us.
And in a cloud of caramel wings,
they came to wrap us in their embrace
as we fought a current that fish could swim against
and tore the bodies from our arms
consumed by a passion we could not understand.

Between Channels

Each noon, all the monks take their place in the square
where Master Po sits in the midst of a vision.
He'll teach them a story, instructing the circle,
before asking for answers from every monk's mouth.
And answers will come till the slow auburn sun
sets, signaling the end of another long day.

Meanwhile, Caine searches a new town each day,
often fighting with gunmen, their jaws hard and square.
He will count the long hours by shadow and sun
and think as he closes his eyes to envision
his master who sits drawing words from his mouth,
who warmly invites him back into the circle.

Elsewhere, an old ranch hand leads his horse in circle.
Little Joe and Hoss head in side for the day,
already the eldest brother has left—his mouth
much too vocal for Ben Cartwright's taste. In the square
Hop Sing works, preparing a meal as his vision
of home stays clouded by a harsh western sun.

At the same time, Kimble sweats under the noon sun,
chased by a big gang that pursues to encircle
his trail. As he runs his mind fills with a vision
of monks telling stories near the end of the day.
Just then, Kimble runs stumbling into the monk's square.
Confused, he stands there, his hand to his mouth.

Gerard interrogates the monks, watching their mouths,
"Why must you seek of him, this fugitive, my son?"
Master Po asks, but Gerard prepares to square
off against Po. Both move to duel in a circle,
as the Fugitive flees off to safety this day,
and Caine steps into Hop Sing's failing vision.

These heroes and villains remain in our vision,
their only wisdom clichés that fall from each mouth,
and their lessons stale syntax left to linger each day
as their cloned, constructed worlds close down when their sun
sets down in the West, to rise in the East. The same circle
repeats—like monks we return to wait in the square.

We live with dimmed vision, under a dim sun
where dim words tumble from dumb mouths.
We circle the set and stare towards the blinding
vacuum of the square.

EDWIN C. EPPS

Baseball Among the Rice Fields

The insistent coarseness of my uniform
in the dead-air heat of August
chafed me as I sat, bench-warmer,
in my second year of Little League,
and as I stood alone,
eighth inning sub,
alert with anticipation upon the right-field grass.
Sweat trickled into the creases of my crotch
alive with jock-itch.
It was the fifties
and wool the fabric that we wore,
a weight against our fielding
that slowed the impulse of my glove
and pulled against my thighs as
back and forth I slow-hopped
in nervous cleats still square and hard,
the thick-scent air tangible
like a cloak-room after rain.

Night.
Top of the inning.
Silence.
The crowd, suspended in the halo of the lights,
a faceless blur of dots,
leaned leftwards toward the plate
where strode my nemesis, behemoth of my dread.
Crrraccckkk!
The kid could hit and hit he did,
a banshee liner right at me.
I watched, a frozen monument to fear itself,

uncertain of my course and its,
and as I stood in speechless wonder there,
the horsehide exploded on my mouth
and smushed my lips onto my astonished teeth,
and down I went.
It was a hit of course.
I lay there unaware
until I saw the face of my ol' coach,
who helped me up to face the brave applause.
My mom, for once attuned to what I prayed,
did *not* approach
in spite of all her instincts must have urged.
Two games on I had a hit
and raised my average up to one for five,
sweet twice a hundred total—
at last I made a contribution to the team.

There was another.
At season's end, we all went out to Ricky's house
where he, an athlete born with instincts, nerve, and grace,
held back as one-on-one we swam a race
and let me win, a feckless kid unused to triumph.
He knew I knew, but neither of us told
and gratefulness was my measure then and now
as I recall when first the weird-sounding name South Vietnam
pushed roughly on my consciousness
and Ricky's name came up among the others,
the ones I didn't know,
the haunting names of all the bright-eyed boys of summer
whose innings ended early when they
were pulled and forced to sit out what
might have been the best damn seasons of their lives.

What the Poet Saw

The rain suspended
up above the ridge,
a bird called soft,
received a husky answer,
and hopped into the sky
for momentary weightlessness,
what brought the poet here at last.

LINDA ANNAS FERGUSON

Living Room, 1956

Because we are too many
for this house, a bed
shares the living room
with a Warm Morning stove.

A photo of the town taken from the air
hangs over the torn vinyl sofa.
All streets lead to the cotton mill,
a gray monument in the middle.
The only world we know is cramped
inside this worn wooden frame.

A seashell lamp from a beach
we've never seen burns for Daddy.
At midnight he will walk home
from second shift,
pour cold coffee, make a sandwich
with an onion and a biscuit.

Tomorrow he will be sleeping
when light wakes us for school,
will leave for work
before we come home again.

We know each other from the warmth
of the fire he stokes for us,
from lessons we study
in the musk of his bed.

Choices

I search through my closet,
try to decide what to wear,
go through the house
luring mirrors to myself.

Clothes make me think of Mama,
hanging wash outside on the line.
Choice to her was a hard wire

stretched across the yard.
When she looks down it,
all she could see was its vanishing point.

She never noticed
how her dresses
danced with the sun,
each to their own rhythm,

the bells of her skirts
capturing the wind, how
her blouses struck poses,
side by side, acting out different lives.

The First Night

As we lie
side by side,
strangers,

my fingers search
your back,
feel the jagged edge

of the rib you gave
in your sleep
to make me.

For this night
I want
to put it back

until I am bone
of your bone
and flesh

of your flesh
and you feel whole again.
In the morning

I will open the wound
so gently
you may not hear me

rise
and tiptoe
out of the garden.

JOAN FISHBEIN

Strictly Personal

I'm pretty   warm   loving fit
a phd social worker
fortyish   spiritual consumer
down-to-earth
I soak up the sun
but my charm heats the room
not high maintenance
I cross-country ski   snow-shoe
skate in-line
sometimes run mini-marathons
stained glass windows
heather flowered
decorate my mountain cabin
so let's connect
if you're between 53 and 67
clean-cut and sassy
savor Louis Armstrong
matzoh balls   abstract art
you can hear my voice
$1.95 per minute
on your touch-tone phone
dial 1-900-lovenow
don't make me buy a bird
I'd rather trip the light fantastic
combine liquid assets with you

STARKEY FLYTHE, JR.

Dogs Closed up in a Room Upstairs for the Party

Three of them. Don't think they don't know, they
slug every Scotch, spread every Triscuit, So and so's
famous salmon dip. They correct the story,
'No, Not Sally, Cynthia, and Pittsburgh,
not Philadelphia.' They stare at each other,
Lab, Corgi, mutt. 'For this,' they snuff,
'we gave up fields, woods, water. The wilds.'
Somebody comes up stairs, their ears point,
the treads squeak, serious bathroom, too serious
for the thin pink powder room walls
downstairs. The dogs, yes, breathe it in.
What that person doesn't know about herself,
her insides. They know the beginning, the end,
the brown between. They're wearing watches,
sense when the party winds down, see
the surreptitious glances, the guests' wrists
under the dining room table, deep breathe
decaf—it is decaf, isn't it? Who'll sleep tonight,
and with whom? Who'll be stopped, going home,
DUI? Sliding through a red light?
Who'll argue who had too much to drink, brought up
dinner, embarrassing gossip? Gaffes.
Who'll stay married, who'll have second thoughts?
Oh, when it's over and they come tearing down,
wagging, sniffing, licking plates, crumbs, and
outside, squatting, legs lifted, the night whimpers
and growls when it all comes out, "Where were you?"
the trees and the wind who also waited whisper.

Mahler Binge

The Boston Symphony Orchestra
has been playing nothing but Mahler, lately,
according to NPR

Crickets, frogs, new music always sounds
like the swamp, like. Where did these notes,
notes in our heads from the beginning come from?
Notes we judge every new sound by?
Like original sin, the first music. No boom boxes
in Eden, cars thumping by, big bass,
only elephant ears, tiger tails, lemur twitters,
animals, all so much smaller then than now
except dinosaurs—why didn't they eat Adam—
answer that, scientists—we know
they didn't eat Eve—all
of them, the smaller the more or less,
why didn't centipedes marry pigs, think
of the hams? All God's creatures
whispering, Call me, I'll come to you.
Dripping wet, breathing fire, a leaf,
a word, a banana will cancel me, slipping,
a bone make or break a saint. Wagner's ego,
swelling in the mud, Brahm's broken bar,
disappearing in Mahler's quicksand. We learn from others,
who read to Adam, his rib, who taught those naked
small-organed, classical bodies? They found,
for we must always be looking, Mahler
in the woods, spirits running, brooks,
seasons, the way rains fall or don't, the way
what is here, what was here, on the grass,
rises, turns to mist and nothing else you still stare after.

CHRIS FORHAN

O.K. Fine

Forgive us our happiness, forgive us
our wacky haircuts, the way we thirst for success
as TV evangelists and high school typing teachers,

letting the crow go silent for want of attention
to his dreary mystery, turning our backs to the sea
repeating unweariedly its one empty gesture.

Forgive us the way we inherited this hallowed ground
and set up shop along the border, avoiding
the dank interior, the way we labor

instructing each other on proper storage
of household combustibles, swapping thoughts
on butter substitutes, wrench sets, sealants,

bleach-based smudge removers—all things solid
by which we're comforted, the way we talk and talk and guard
our hearts, our pure and idiot middle, believing

life is a gift to earn by not letting on
our desire for it. This is O.K. This is fine.
We're plenty astonished. Summer's come, shuffling in

like a laid-off textile worker. Radio towers
rise like pines through the mist behind
the convenience store. Its white sign

stutters on as dawn arrives, tipping
its lavender hat, settling a light on each pelican
lawn ornament and pink concrete garden frog.

There's always something. The frocked bishop wiggling, relieving
an itch. A doll's arm gnawed by a dog at the edge
of the park. A wig in the road. We're plenty astonished.

A Sickly Child

Loosed from the womb, I swooned
on my first breath. The doctor
urged me into this world
with a kiss to my still lips.

Each of my bristling sisters
slipped her skates off and tiptoed
in stocking feet to pass my door.
I was given much medicine
from large blue bottles.

The blinds were always drawn
and my windows cracked an inch
in summer. Often I drowsed,
the dull sound of weeping or whispering
in the hall, or one of my brothers
calling my name from the darkening street.

Grandmother, wigged and recoiling
from the stench, occasionally entered
my room at Christmas, leaving me
big books to prop on my chest.
Legends of the living dead.
Adventures of a sightless orphan
and his mongrel dog. Tales
of the martyred child saints.

Also, sometimes, late afternoons—mother
stooped in the kitchen, straining a cauldron
of steaming soup for me; father
alone in the basement stuffing
swansdown into immense pillows
for my bed—I'd slip out
to the neighbor kid's, Eddie O'Shaughnessy,
who'd beat me bloody
and tell me to get over it.

The Vastness. The Distant Twinkling

When the Great Unknowable One shook out
the immaculate tablecloth of the stars,
concealing all the while the sight
of his own magnificence, we applauded.
We kept this up for some time. What else

could we do? What words could we speak
in reply? Oh, it was past all comprehension.
The vastness. The distant twinkling. The simple
inexplicableness of the trick. Ourselves there
to witness. A wonder, we told each other, to be sure,

but with something a little sad about it.
At last, our hands numb from clapping,
each of us slipped his hat on, waved so long,
and went his solitary way. We were hungry
and we had a few things to think about.

RICHARD GARCIA

These Moments

The sky this evening over Charleston,
just dramatic enough to say, *it's good*—
strolling across the parking lot while the sun
lights up the bottom of clouds as you
are on your way to Taco Bell. Those clouds
remind you of a tromp-l'oeil crepuscule
in Las Vegas that makes you believe
you are sitting by a canal in Venice
in the early evening. The gondoliers
in their striped shirts drift along the shore.
O *Sole Mio*. The sky nostalgic, wisps of cirrus
seem to drift across it. You ask to sit outside,
because this is one of those moments, even if this
is not Venice, even if you're really indoors.

The White Ghosts

White ghosts were ruining the neighborhood
like an army of blank real estate signs
like refrigerators abandoned on front lawns
that were really graveyards.
This occurred to me while I took a shower
with the sister of my former wife.
She was so afraid of the white ghosts,
she wore her bathing suit
and over that, her dark blue dress.
I wrote this down on her dress
with a pen that had white, waterproof ink.
I wanted to write more about the white ghosts
so I peeled her dress off.
She liked that and kissed me,
sticking her tongue into my mouth.
Her tongue was not soft and warm
but stiff and cool like cardboard,
and tasted like a communion wafer.
Then I lay next to you thinking,
it's good I brought her dress with me
so I could write about the white ghosts.
Then I thought, you fool, you can't carry
things out of a dream, so forget about
the white ghosts. I got up and took
my dog to the park but he would not
get out of the car. I don't know for sure,
but I think the field was full of white ghosts,
and he could see them standing there,
silent, like the ghosts of a Ku Klux Klan meeting.
White noise is not white.
White chocolate is not chocolate.
Avalanches are not soft and fluffy.
When I got home, the ghost
of a white pit bull was writhing
on the kitchen floor, whining and sliding
toward me across the linoleum on her belly.

Eradication of Exotic Pets

Sometimes in the middle of the night
I am interviewed by a lovely young girl.
She has red hair and creamy skin.
What do you think of the world she asks?
I answer: You know when you're falling in love
but are afraid to let the one you love
know it because you're afraid they'll disappear?
She nods, looking up at me, brushes
her hair back from her forehead.
Well, that's how I feel about the world.
She bows her head, scribbles in her notebook.
Sometimes in the middle of the night
my soul gets tired of being two people
and, knowing I don't care for the tropics,
flies off to Hawaii. Sometimes in the middle
of the night I meet a young woman,
perhaps she's a hooker and I'm a cab driver.
I'm taking her around to different hotels.
She looks out the cab window. No, she says,
and I keep driving. It's a slow night
for cab drivers and hookers. Finally
she gives me an address in El Segundo.
It's a tract house. She pays, tips nicely, gets out.
I start to head back, that's when I notice
a sheet of paper on the rear seat.
I assume it's my next poem but apparently
it's for Richard Garcia the entomologist.
It's the title page to his next book,
Eradication of Exotic Pests.
Sometimes in the middle of the night
I wait on the beach while my soul goes surfing.
She strides out of the water carrying her board.
Look, she says, handing me a shell
that resembles a petrified, crumbled piece of paper,
and she gives me that Veronica Lake,
Audrey Hepburn, half tomboy, half vixen smile.

STEPHEN GARDNER

Jones

"This shaking keeps me steady"

The rainfall has been steady for so long
it seems heavier than it is, connected
with fine wire to my itchy fingertips.
Tonight, I pray to be pure water,
to go where it can go: last night
I dreamed myself a river that can choose
without gravity its own course.

I'm holding on like death to something
shriveled up inside me, my nails
cracked, skin dry, yet all the while
I tremble as if this leather chair could be
slightly seismic. I can't make you
understand the need for such a fix,
but there's no anger here, only fire

in the belly and a heart that may just stop.
On the coffee table, I've arranged water,
dropper, matches, and an empty spoon.
The candle's burning, half-way down, and Bix
is blowing out a tune. The blinds are drawn,
and all the lights are out. I'm on the floor,
leaning against the couch, waiting for you.

I'm Waiting for the Milk Truck

that hasn't been through here
for over 25 years,
that young driver, him with his
starched and pearly-white shirt
and pants, white shoes, curt black
bowtie, toting right-handed
the gray wire basket of bottles,
six, barely clinking,
with their paper tops, setting
them on the stoop, retrieving
the empties; and, if he saw my mother
seeing him through the kitchen window,
he'd give a small nudge to his square
white cap that said PET MILK, nod,
duck his head, chin to chest,
and step up into the white PET truck
and drive, yes, drive next door,
where I'm not.

Waiting to Leave

Even when the owls retreat to their nests
You cannot sleep. And like the hunting eyes
Of foxes, you stare too long into the dark
So that in time you know you are alone.
What can be felt is of another world:

The burn of feline eyes into your back,
Silent feet on straw, the wind at peace
With the trees. It is a world resting tonight,
Except for you. Dreaming awake, you feel
Your hand on the suitcase grip, the crush and pull

Of strangers running to distant gates,
The voices, hard and polished in the air,
Announcing the arrivals. Then you tilt
Your head back, bracing underneath your neck
With sweaty wrists, and stare: the ceiling rolls

In nightmare visions. Smoke rings from distant fires
Curl and twist together. Trouble is brewing
On the prairie. The deer watch motionless as trees.
The lynx stands sudden guard beside her kill.
And then your woman shifts her back to you.

Her breathing holds the silence on its edge.
And there the foxes sit. Their eyes stare back,
Then wink, then fade away, running at the sound
Of twigs that snap to footsteps not your own.
You know you can't return before you've gone.

GEORGE P. GARRETT

Shards for Her

You are the spirit dancing in seven veils.
(I watch you from my bed of nails.)

You know the deep places of the sea.
You know the dance of fountains in the light.
You are the spirit dancing in seven veils.

You breathe the keen air of mountains.
You have seen the glare of heatstricken, silent places.
(I see you from my bed of nails.)

You bring me the green heart of springtime.
I taste. It is bitter and good.
You are the spirit dancing in seven veils.

You are all my light
when I wrestle with angels and daemons.
Come, love me on a bed of nails.

Giant Killer

I've heard the case for clarity. I know
much can be said for fountains and for certain bells
that seem to wring the richness from the day
like juice of sweetest fruits, say, plums and tangerines,
grapes and pineapples and peaches. There are so many
ripe things, crushed, will sing on the thrilled tongue.

I know the architecture of the snow's composed
of multitudes of mirrors whose strict forms
prove nothing if they do not teach that God loves all
things classic, balanced and austere in grace
as, say, Tallchief in *Swan Lake*, a white thing floating
like the feather of a careless angel, dropped.

But there are certain of God's homely creatures that
I can love no less—the shiny toad, a fine hog fat in mud,
sporting like Romans at the baths, a mockingbird
whose true song is like oboes out of tune, a crow
who, cawing above a frozen winter field,
has just the note of satire and contempt.

I will agree that purity's a vital matter,
fit for philosophers and poets to doze upon. I'll agree
the blade is nobler than a rock. But then I think
of David with Goliath, how he knelt
and in a cloudy brook he felt for stones.
I like that disproportion. They were well thrown.

Gray on Gray

Risen shades   thin shadows   coats and layers
of glare ice   frozen slush   patches of old snow
and the wide slack moronic yawning horizon
shabby waste of woodsmoke overflowing   falling
heavy to be lazy scattered by the pale wind
where I'm walking squinting   leaning into it
breathing it deeply in   myself wrapped in rags
of gray thought   talking to myself
myself a yawning stranger   gray on gray

CECILE GODING

In the Nursing Home

Let there be light
in this corridor fluorescent with wheelchairs.

Give us this day
central air conditioning, and chocolate.

Deliver us from
fishforks, foundation garments, RSVPs.

And forgive us our
cattiness, our medals, gilt brooches.

As we forgive
bruises, raised eyebrows, cold peas.

Haloed be the one
who will spoon me my last meal.

For she has rowed me
across the dance floor with her voice.

Taking Down Sheets at Night

Around me, clean walls. Above me, no roof
unless you count stars. In the nearby hospital,
a child is born while another one expires.
My neighbor steps out on her porch to smoke—
she's that red coal rising and falling, now gone.
Between us, white clover on this buried farm.
Nothing else, we've never swapped names.
Wasn't that the sound of her new wind chimes?
Nothing else, unless you count stars.
Into a wicker basket, I drop wooden pins
and all. Soon I'll have the whole house down.

Yankee Doodle

When there was nothing but the horseshoe
of crumbling Gothic church, block-long city hall,
and tower of finance, she was innocent.
She stood there shouting sermons in her plywood
scripture sandwich, words distorted
by wind and a life of hollering Jesus,
ending with a tune, a whistled doxology
funneling quickly out on Boylston or down a subway vent.
Before the Navaho welders leaped
along these girders, transforming floors to ceilings,
before fantasy suites rose on cranes
to carpeted space on upper levels, until the last
shiny curtain-wall was bolted into place,
she never knew how terrible she sounded.
But now, in the plaza recently squared
by an advertising firm, every note reverberates
off all that brick and chrome and glass,
and she realizes she's been off key,
especially that last i in Macaroni, all these years,
and no one ever told her.
        But still, she believes
that by some property of physics, even a warped "Yankee Doodle"
rises, like underwater screaming, up smooth
aluminum sides to where the people sit. She imagines they stop
chowing down on take-out deli bagels, and halt
brain-busting searches for the newest slant on cereal.
They look around at each other.
So what if they smirk a little?
They are waiting for her to finish,
but for years she whistles on, like a dolphin in a pool,
swimming lazily around, keeping his sonar going.
We know now that it hurts, this bouncing off
concrete and his own eroding brain.
What he hopes for is anything.

VERA GÓMEZ

Cafeteria Food

The daily nickel marked me.
I'd take it from my pinned coin purse
to pay for the pint of Quality Check milk.
I carried a brown bag, tattered from use
and freckled by oil spot stains.
They had full trays and lunch cards.
My solitary bag stood tall—it's mouth open.
Their flesh-toned trays lined tabletops.

My spicy tacos permeated the air.
Unwrapping the reused Reynolds Wrap,
I'd look down and wish I were white.
Wish I had bologna on Wonder bread.
Wish I could forsake the taste of *chorizo*—
but I was hungry. I'd here the kids whisper,
Spick. I'd think *pinche gringos*, like
Papi when he was mad at the world.

The room's ordinary wall resembled
the English my tongue would learn to flap.
Back when I longed for rolled *Rs* and spoken
syllables accented and topped by tildes.
But in the school cafeteria only *wows* and
way *cools* echoed. My *chorizo* tacos and chocolate
milk learned to speak for themselves.

ALY GOODWIN

In November

for L.

I bring dogwood buds inside to force-bloom
believing they hold secrets
living as tightly-wound coils deep inside cocoons
without forethought or grief.

If I could be part of something, only a part,
I'd be dogwood buds filling vases
in rooms of a house like mine, house of the heart
and secret places.

If I could be a part of something I'd choose
one hand-forged nail in a chestnut fence on Bald Face
Mountain, where invisible stars rise over a pale blue lake

or the scent of Mongolian tea whispering *ginger*
or brine borne on a sea-wind

The Hook

for L.

The smell of today's fresh
newspaper
nudges a feeling
inside and unmined
and which
I can't name.
Help me with it:

what do I call childhood,
sitting in my Father's lap
opening the paper together
and pulling out the comics?
His clothes smell of Turkish
tobacco and the oh, so fine
newsprint
as he reads *Dagwood
Bumstead* and *Popeye*
then walks
to the second
floor and down
to the first floor
and out the
door
and is gone into memory,
a hook embedded
in a fish who can't name it,
a book
handed to someone
who will only, but swiftly,
close it.
How would the fish
explain the hook?

*It is like
swimming
under the roof of all sadness
in an old, submerged tabernacle.*

LAUREN GOULD

Please, Do Not Touch

The octipetal flower   a pinwheel
                                or glance over coarse
water
to a long stem. Colors like this love the bellies of chrysanthemums,

and despite seasons of dearth,
rain dances are eternal. The caption says:

Two cotton ceremonial squares
hand embroidered with silk floss
Swat, Pakistan
Gift of Mrs. Ben Eaton
29 ¾ x 27
31 x 29 ¾

And what if you wrapped the squares like sisters around your shoulder
blades?
                                Who would stop
you?
Clara Ray with her navy museum uniform and name badge.

It's cold in here, you tell her. On second thought,
I was just putting these back.

          There's truth in the way you keep being alive.
First, out of habit
                        and then for being told
no.

LINDSAY GREEN

Thank Sylvia

for thinking to situate a dishcloth between her cheek
and the oven rack, preferring puffed plum knees
on the kitchen floor to ditches of grease
stripes on her fair complexion;

for mimicking her passport picture
with hot-red Vogue lips and glassy,
tucked-under blonde hair,
for hoarding and re-ordering her pink stationery paper,
for biting on the first date;

and for the first attempt—
because I'm not enterprising enough
to check my breath and paranoia
in a dank earth-womb, incubating like a virus under the house,
moaning into the walls for three days;

for being the wife instead of the large-eyed mistress,
and for not knowing the difference,
and for acting as if she did;

for evoking babies in jars and on shelves,
for daddies rotting at the end of a path in nightmares,
for countering with domestic genius,
peeling apples and potatoes.

Disparity

Slinking under bushes and street
lamps and porches of strangers,
she holds the concrete
against her stomach.
She can look in the mirror,
break it, then eat it again.
She has written her lover's
poem a thousand times.

She does not consider
the boundaries of bodies,
does not fight her own.
She can breathe.
She is not a visionary—
no flashing play and rewind

films of blood in the drain,
hair matted on the ground,
young women dressed in white,
or umbilical cords still fresh
in their own juices.

She does not take the chunks
of beautiful she can get
in the back of her throat.
She can give birth to it,
dress it in lace and a hat,
hold its hand in the park,
and not drop it.

Throwing Apples

I.
My fistful of clouded half-memories
clink and roll against each other
like marbles in my throat.
I retrieve them from a muffled pocket,
to roll them around
in my palm like I should,
to inspect their weather-worn
hues and temperature, to retouch
and preserve any cracks or chinks,
because the last day of October is always his.

II.
All I have to show are three
squat little apples, mismatched
and overripe, sleeping sparrows
nestled together, balancing
on a taut telephone line,
punctuating the barely-dark sky.
I can fit all three on one hand;
their waxy skins brush and catch
as they rub cheek to cheek,
as they rock back and forth
and bruise easily as babies' heads.

III.
I thought I could pitch them across
the one-way street, all of them pressed
together in a strain-claw grip.
One made it, barely off the shoulder
and into a scrub oak, while the others
bounced once and stopped, chunked and lustrous,
two half-tasted moons charted in the road.
I retrieved them like I should,
full of chinks and juice dripping
from my knuckles, because the last day
is always his, always barely-dark and bruised.
I couldn't leave them there.

BEN GREER

Death Among Friends

for Marhsa

Now is the bleak inception of your mortal end.
For years I envisioned this moment—
about who would first hear the physician's comment:
I'm sorry. It's cancer. Are you her friend?

Afterwards, I just drove around for half the day.
Then something else inexplicable: a brown
cloud descended. I felt as if I might drown
in the strange, sudden stench. Wild fires burning in May.

I was surprised to be so completely shaken.
We are sixty, seasoned, but I was mistaken
to think that I could calmly accept the news

and balance my checkbook or work-out or day dream
about anything. Brown and still, the gripping hours teem
with pictures of you, of me, of all we lose.

A Teacher's Discovery

I would not let you fall in love with me
though you wanted to because of what I found:
music. The craze and crack of your words
I read that winter morning I will always
hear. And because I told you: look,
look at this. Look at what you have done.
Incredible. Your hands grabbed mine and brought
them to your mouth wet as half a peach
to kiss, knowing the agonies
of your life now had meaning: a poem
with such incomprehensible edge
that all who press it open and bleed
at last understanding their own sickness,
spilling it out luxuriously,
pouring it out hotly, madly, dreamily
until there is only one sense remaining:
the emptiness of the healed.

L.L. HARPER

My love

My love is a gnawed apple, cavalierly tasted, tossed to the grass, left to the
ants and worms, the wetblack night. He is as talkative as a wrist, the odor of
his shame after fucking, pungent, almost a color. His old lover haunts me,
a rabid terrier stalking a rabbit. I feel the giddy tarantula of delight spread
across my face when I learn of her demise. I am no saint. No stigmata
rises like Braille across my hands when U pump him hard as a '57 T-Bird's
pistons oiled well. As artful, as ephemeral as a blown kiss, my jealousy
ducks light. Her death, an ugly truth, releases nothing, her hold on both of
us, gravely dexterous. But loathsome as love's cowardice, his capitulation
to the here and now excites me. Watch out. I am a conscientious moon
harnessed to the tides like an ass plowing the beaches. If you swim these
waters, I tell him to his second face, you better not need to come up for air.
I am the only air you need. He smiles, a shark circling, diving deeper.

Grandfather Hothead

Hagan fell asleep
with a burning cigarette
you hunted down like
a hound vixen in heat.
Vain as an intellectual
closing in on his main point,
sure it won't be missed,
impossible to misconstrue,
you split your knuckles
setting Hagan straight.
His jaw cracked, the sound
like a fox's leg snapping
in a boxtrap.

Wire, Hagan sipped supper
for two months and you,
Grandfather Hothead,
accent thick as your arm,
roofer, sheet-metal worker,
brute, drunk, defeated,
you blended beef and potatoes,
liver and onions stinking as sweat,
stew, greens, and cake, sweet
as chocolate to pulp, then creamed
the mess for Hagan and his straw,
paper proboscis, arsonist anteater,
who two years later would burn
the whole basement with one
cigarette smoldering under a bed.
For years, Hagan, jaw cemented shut
behind his charred smile,
danced in the blender,
smoky ghost,
Grandfather Hothead's
little worm of conscience.

Rusted tractor

On the back plat of the acreage
we find it grounded in flood waters
the old stream swells to this spring.

As antiquated as the ethical canon
we left in the city, I want its wheels
to plant in a swell of black dirt,

to seed mandevilla and clematis
around its spokes, urge the tendrils
to wrap each rusted circle in a festivity

of tortured vines flaming with fleshy trumpets
hummingbirds, compulsive as despots, would love.
You conquer mercies the way you

batter tenderness and so refuse
to deconstruct it, and when you try
to pull it out of the water to sell

to Dex for scrap, it disassembles itself,
chassis thudding into the mud,
a gear box and drive shaft

halved by a boulder under its hood
which unfolds like a desiccated wing
and crashed down loud as a combine stopping.

I tell you that's what you get
for being mean and you,
new to this political fairway of disgrace,

take me out for dinner that night,
buy wine to take home,
wash my hair and brush it dry,

ignore our plug poverty,
make love as satisfying as a pocket
bulging with cash, plant cornflowers

out by the mailbox, and morning glories.
They will rise on twine all the way
to the roof later this summer,

that high, all the way up.

MELANIE G. HARRIS

In Rooms Like This

Somewhere in a room
like this one
with a floral print spread
on the one bed, a Gideon Bible
and a TV with HBO, your leather case
rests on a hard plastic counter.
Your one expensive suit hangs
on an open rack. You are there
unbuttoning, unzipping
adeptly
    undressing a woman
you do not love.
She is letting you use her up.
And men in little rooms
just like this
are at this hour
in towns
like this
stripping women
down to the bones
they will not cherish
while their wives
wait at home, satisfied
they have had
their goodnight calls.

The Next Time

The next time I see
the light in a young man's eyes
the hint of desire
I'll remember a phone number
scribbled in the dark
and won't be persuaded
to believe what is past
can be given again.
I'll keep my pen in my pocket
smile and say thank you,
remembering the place
I tried to return to
and found unreachable.

The night does not hold
what the light in a young man's eyes
promise, so I will forget you held me
talked to me in your sweet low voice.

And when I'm tempted
to listen again to sweet low voices
I will remember what I feel now
and know even such sweetness
is not worth some pain.

In Yellowstone Park, Fires Burn Out of Control

Forest fires rage around the mountain village
where you live, in an enclave of music.
I imagine the day of your birth
your mother holding you and naming you, Adam,
formed of Earth, in God's image,
after his likeness. She had all hope for you
believed all things.   In the fire
of earth's beginnings, you were there.
Belief did not fail her. With your flute
you name grief and define longing.
Now, from Cincinnati, she calls
tries to get through jammed lines,
to hear your voice, to know
the fires have not reached you.

She is not the only woman who worries.
Did she know when she named you
that you would call Eves to your side.
Did she fear? Didn't she know in her faith
How you would be desired. Did she hope for it?
Was she ready to let you leave her arms
to crawl, then walk into manhood and the desires
of women who want to hold you, and name
you again in the darkness, "Adam, Adam—"

MARGARET B. HAYES

Illusion

Two sand dollars, a broken whelk
and an empty scallop shell
laid out like corpses
on a plain, white porch,
lie silent as bleached bones
picked clean by vultures.
Deprived of rolling water
and pulsing breakers,
they are sad reminders they don't
belong here,
and I keep trying to
hold onto something that
slips through my fingers
like dry sand.

JANNETTE HYPES

Naming Bogotá

I was six and didn't understand
Why God put gold in the ground.
My father was a jeweler
For sixteen years before deciding
There was more gold in Bogotá.
He said he didn't take to selling
Himself short, said "that's how
You know a man."
His hip pocket showed white
Where he packed his brown leather
Wallet. Mamma said he never used it,
That's why. I remember waving him
Away to Bogotá; hearing him say
My a hands were gypsy's.
I fold them now—plain, simple and empty.

Because This Is the Time

To plant, I kneel among brittle stalks
Of snapdragons, sweep away ribbons
Of leaves. Because I have unearthed the winter
Worm, placed it between gloved fingers,
Watched it turn inside its tight skin,
I have learned to speak softly to the ground:
"The plants are in love with their roots."

The man next door comes out
For his saw. The screen door bounces
Twice behind him then twice again.
He is working wood, making his own
Shape, carving loose scenes of wise men.
Inside, the kettle is boiling, the wife hurries
In her cotton slippers. I am digging

A home for the cuttings, waiting for the words
That will tell if he takes lemon or honey or cream.
"You can live here," I tell the hyacinth and settle
the bulb in its hollow. Today, it is lemon.
The house settles down to spoons.

Tea steams in the glow of a yellow kitchen,
In mugs held between aged hands. I pack
The dirt hard with the face of my palm
And sit back on the roots of my feet.

Where I Am From

Cows lie down, and I know before
Rain comes. Clouds milk the sky,

Turn gray, fall; in this light, even scrub
oaks look beautiful. I want to be patient,

a cow on a dusky hill, golden-pink
like the faces of children waking.

I want to be beautiful for a time,
An oak turning gay on the face of a hill.

I want to fall down in the rain
And lie there waking.

THOMAS L. JOHNSON

The Artist's Subject

—On Hassam's "The Green Gown"
in Gibbes Museum, Charleston

Monsieur, hélas, that you have caught me at this
season: out of sorts and indisposed
to art of any kind—or, for that matter,
thought and feeling. Can't see how I'd bring
myself to pose for you, or anybody else,
right now. Don't have the heart or stomach
for it. If by chance you made a lovely
work of me through your superb technique,
so that my portrait wound up hung in some
salon for months, or in the galleries for years,
how could I stand to be exposed to every
critic's take on me? And they'd be right:
I have no face to speak of—just a mask,
a Greek thing made of stone; my hair's a mess,
of course (you think I give a fig for how
it looks?); my posture says I'm either lost
or lazy, maybe both. Beneath my gown,
my bones don't fit my feet. But worst of all,
my hands: each one can only hold on to
the other for dear life, or pity's sake.

                     If you insist, however,
I will do it on these three conditions:
that you paint me only in a dress
which swallows me alive—the one I wore
the night I met him years ago, a green
affair decked out in roses; that you seat me
in the foyer on the fancy bench
before my gorgeous oriental screen,

the one in gold whose black-winged birds
now seem to dive and swoop to peck out both
my eyes; and then, to match the number of those
birds, you'll have to find a pot of tulips
in the favorite color of my dear
Van Gogh, to place beside me for some beauty
and some life, to brighten up the space
and speak sweet hope these winter days.
Be sure to come back soon, Monsieur,
before I change my mind.

The Grave of Abdul Aziz al-Saud

Since they refused to mark your grave,
perhaps at your own word, we do
not make long treks to visit any
mosque or pile of rocks which say
you lie just there. But we know where
you are. The sand is always in our
eyes. It takes no special storm
to force inside our lids enough,
and more, to make us cry each day.
The desert life is one long living
grief: we weep to wash you out,
to cleanse from sight your flesh and bone.
You saw, and knew, that if you had
no tomb you would not die, but make
survivors water your dry earth—
yourself—with their own constant flood
of tears, and maybe with their blood.

A Southern Boy Reflects on Miss Monroe

What did they do to you out there?
If you had been a Southern girl
you could have come back home
and bought the town, and you'd have
owned us all—and you'd have had
a place where stars are still
those first things in the night
we make wishes on, and spring
when it returns each year brings
innocence once more, and blossoms
on the trees retain the power to blush
when touched. After all, you've had
our hearts already, in the sense that
Ashley meant when he attempted to respond
to Scarlett's blatant declaration of her
love for him. You would have been
assured of quiet, diligent attention:
we'd have called you "Ma'm" and gently
opened doors for you, but also seen to it
you were protected by a pattern of reserve
which does not dare intrude upon the shadows
palms and louvers make on summer beds or
chaises underneath a lazy fan. You could
have checked out *Light in August* from the
old maid in the shotgun house which serves
as public library, or read *Camille* out
underneath the live oak on the courthouse
square, and no one would have thought it
odd. And when you died—perhaps of boredom
rather than of grief, despair, and loneliness—
we would have softly sung, "Come home, come
home" for you and for ourselves, and dug
your grave beneath the towering magnolia
in the cemetery's heart, where you would

never fail to be surrounded by eternal
green, the scent of blooms in spring,
the generous applause of leaves which
love to fall before the feet of tragic
beauty gone to earth. But there, out
there: what did they do for you?

ANGELA KELLY

Voodoo Doll

The body could fit in a palm. A cup of the hand.
Piece-meal, the scraps glued or quilted quickly,
but enough to know it is her body.
The arms, the torso, fashioned from her favorite day-gown,
the satin legs from a filched negligee,
the button-eye head holds a lock of her hair,
blonde strands plucked from a sable hairbrush,
and the feet, though toeless, turn slightly outward
as her own are prone to do.

And if this voodoo doll could walk,
it would glide and strut just as I have seen her do so
in a room full of men.
            And which is my father?   I ask her
with a pin here, a pin there.   *Which?*
But her porcupine self does not answer.

From the servant's quarter stairs I spy
into the parlor, worn velvet and wallpaper of nymphs.
I look into the face of each man and I think
of the cufflinks and coins, the ties and handkerchiefs,
all the things that fall from their pockets
as they sit on the couches, waiting, with thin dollars,
sipping tumblers of watered-down whiskey,
perhaps teasing the girl in garters, already on their laps.

I climb the steps to my bed in the attic and
I think to make a voodoo man next,
not in answer to her, but simply to make something better,
his shoulders stronger, his legs thicker,
that wallet on his backside filled with good dollars,
his chest marked by an indigo heart of disappearing ink.

Up Worry Hut

The ATF agents came looking for Rudolph
up Worry Hut. They found rhododendron thickets.
They shouldered M-16s and wore camouflage
against the green hell of the high mountains.
Worry Hut let them in, and then swallowed them
like it has everything else, the Mississippians,
the Cherokee, Old Rob's great grandfather
who rode a mule up the hollow the first time.

College students in trailers near the mouth
didn't stop the agents. They came on up the hollow
past the last Floridians who build on the view lot ridges,
on up to where Old Rob and his people have lived
since the settlement. There's two water crossings
to get to Old Rob's land, and a bend in the road
so deep it will put a crease in any car longer than
a wagon. Old Rob still likes it that way.

Old Rob says he's seen an Indian princess
up in a laurel sprawl high near the parkway.
He's heard her brown baby cry too. On Worry Hut
such sounds blend with the slow rain, the luna moth's
wings at night, the salamander leaving a watery
trail through the falling branch. "He could be
under any stone," Old Rob says of Rudolph.
"He could be hole up in some hidden Indian cave."
Up Worry Hut, anything's possible. The road goes
nowhere but higher. The forest grows greener
and deeper with each twisted mile of two track.

Some say there's little people up Worry Hut,
from before the Indians. Building one house
a man with a backhoe opened up tiny little
tunnels all over the hill side, perfectly round
and only four feet high. He told no one but me,
not out of fear as much as respect for the mystery.

See that curling tail of rock dust? That's
the government men leaving Worry Hut.
Rob knows they'll be back, but not today or tomorrow.

They looked for Indians like Tsali up here,
taxes, Confederate conscripts, and corn whiskey.
Found nothing but the lonesome call of the hoot owl,
the circle of the dogwood blossom, the drooping
trillium in bloom all over Worry Hut in the spring.

Old Rob's Last Allotment

1.
When winter grabbed hold of Worry Hut
Old Rob piled the year's brush
in long rows, lit the dry locust branches,
withered maple saplings, the tops of stove
wood oaks. The dead wood caught.
As the last pile flamed out, Rob watched
grey ash swirling in the wind like snow.

2.
Burly Knob humped beyond Rob's field,
seemed ready to bend under February cold.
Dry weeds from last year's season covered
rock piles in the quarter acre field
Rob's son still let him plant in the old ways.

3.
Ash killed the seeds of weeds sleeping below.
In March Rob started seeds, tearing open each
government pack, Kentucky 101 and Tennessee.
In the barn he filled little Dixie Cups with dark
hollow earth pushed each seed thumb deep.

4.
Rob's mule was old as he was, moved
slow in the rising heat after the last frost.
When May showed they moved one last time
together between the rock piles, broke the land,
prepared the bottom field for the last planting.

The Locust

Old Rob lived his life with the persistence
of locust. He was like an old post set deep
in a dark hole, the bark long gone.
The durability of his mountain days
was no different than the rafters in his
'bacca barn, the stakes he shaped to
hold his springy stock fence.

Before Rob died he counted
his grandchildren, like little locust
sprouts in his backfield, the fallow one
where the cattle can't graze.
They grow up every summer
paying no heed to the absence of shade.
Sprouts, runners from Rob's line,
pushing out green leaves and black thorns.

The honey of Rob's days was dark
like that spun by black bees
in April from the long white blooms.
When Old Rob died his casket was made
from a big locust the wind brought down
at the end of Worry Hut. He told his son,
"Cut broad boards at the sawmill,
join 'em good. I'll be happy when the time
comes, sunk deep in that dark locust box."

THOMAS DAVID LISK

March 20, 2002

All day a spook like blood has lingered in my upper throat,
halfway between taste and smell, tantalizing, both

because, while faintly medicinal, it's not an evil flavor,
and because I can almost say it without metaphor–

the smell of iodine, a whiff of wet salt, the taste of rare beef–
and, though it appears ghostly in my feelings,

because it's not *like* something else, it has a firm identity
compounded of smells and tastes. Or it's as if there is no "reality,"

only metaphor, and I feel whatever it is connects
with the mysterious coincidences

in W. G. Sebald's books, *The Emigrants*, *The Rings of Saturn*,
         Austerlitz
(which I have been reading one after another),

as if the fleeting taste of *Vertigo* made physical were floating in my
         throat,
answering disintegration with an early olfactory ghost.

In the Book Hotel

In the book hotel, a box
with paper walls and fabric
wainscoting, I rubbed dark
leather, complaining about
wasted light. There was so
much around, so much unread.
I was after something
thick and durable, not
close-ordered letters
overwhelmed by light, too grim
to be magnificent. Here were
my moments, my transactions,
my conviction that these
volumes used as multi-colored
bricks for an identity castle
entirely shingled with black
bibles held in the end
no trace of me, a temporary
occupant made to make and justify
these blue innumerable dreams.

Between Earth and Sky

1. Mother

In "American Portrait Old Style,"
when Robert Penn Warren speaks

of "a Plymouth Rock or maybe a fat Dominecker
that fell to the crack of the unerring Decherd,"

I ache for his experience to be mine,
young imagination killing real hens,

but I never killed a blessed thing
with my lever-action air carbine.

I pinged at robins, jays and grackles
who flew away cackling,

single copper beads dripping from their armor feathers
while I punctured nothing, but drew the mild wrath

of a burley State trooper nicknamed Chink
who peered through the screen at our verandah door.

Frightened by his length and broad flat hat
pinch-rumpled to a stiff point,

what could I do but cringe apology
and be relieved he didn't confiscate my gun,

the only little gift my father gave
that didn't disappear or break.

My lonely mother, who liked the tall cop's kindly face,
saw "punishment enough" in my dark gaze.

2. Father

When my sobered father took his belt
to me it was not for dinging glass or birds

but for a time I couldn't stop
myself and on a wet spring day popped

a single hole in the shiny rubber boot
of a younger kid I thought of as a boob,

a cruelty of mine that now confuses me
because I hate to think how—thoughtless, weirdly free—

I must have held the cocked toy rifle pressed against
his yellow toe cap belly and squeezed the trigger,

and after the pumped-air's muffled cough
I lifted the muzzle from a little BB hole

as if a copper worm had burrowed in his toe.
Though everything inside the boot was whole,

his shiny new protection leaked. No Chink came,
and my feckless dad had no one but me to blame

for whatever shame he must have felt
when the wronged boy's mother yelled.

But still, some days I woke with joy
and dreamed awake this weapon toy

quick-charged with air I drew myself
was really capable of murder.

SUSAN LUDVIGSON

The Lilies of Landsford Canal

Twenty years I've lived
    so near a miracle
        it's possible to bicycle there.

(Not me, so out of shape a walk up a long hill leaves me
breathless, but my fit neighbor says so.)

In canoes we navigate the stony shoals,
    shores and islands green
        as a long-remembered dream.

But where are the promised lilies?

I thought they'd be like Monet's,
    floating flat at the edge of a river
        under the shadow of willows bending
            to riffle the water.

The others think we must be too late, must have missed
    the season.

A few clumps of tall grasses
    have stalks with possible buds, or maybe
        they're the stubble of flowers now blown

    by the wind toward shore,

    but in any case, there's nothing like blooms
anywhere.

Then we round a bend and there they are—choirs

swaying in a rhythm to the moving water.

They are singing hosannas, a music

so ecstatic and silent it has to be white.

Whole islands are massed with them, long stems and dark
            embracing leaves like French genets,
but the delicate spiked white blossoms are enormous
            and complex

as stars through a telescope. They shine against
            the skittering silver water,
                against the trembling wall of green behind,
                    against the stones rising up

in the shallows, seeming, by contrast, fragile.

But no.
                    They grow wild
            in just a few places in the world.

A thousand years old, against the odds,
            they repeat themselves year after year

                like swallows or salmon returning home.

I rarely enter anything like their world.

Even when we're past

            that shimmering, the Catawba wider
                and smoother than before, the air is fragrant

as a childhood summer.

Surely there is no more innocence here than anywhere.
Downstream, I'm told, the river is polluted by chemicals.

Yet I feel as if I'm entering something pure,
       some place not wholly exterior. I knew it once,
         I think, but so long ago it has ceased to be.

Islands of lilies live so close
       I could have watched them open
          every year.

I could have kept them where closed eyes
       would bring them back, white plumes
         soothing the air.

For twenty summers

I could have picnicked on these and other banks

       where canoes glide by, some of their passengers, like me,
       late discovering their lives.

Bin Laden in South Carolina

"It is equal to living in a tragic land
To live in a tragic time."
                    Wallace Stevens

We are strolling near the forest when we spot him.
You aim your rifle, he puts his hands up so slowly
he seems to be starting to dance, a dance that begins
in his graceful fingers.

We march him to our house in the meadow,
to the backyard where you tie him
to a chair.

I bring him books. *Bind his wrists if you must,*
I plead, *but please leave his hands free enough*
to turn the pages. You do not acknowledge
that you've heard me.
I shrug in his direction, reassuring.

I wonder if he reads English.
He must be bored, I say, *sitting in the sun*
for hours. I think of lemonade,
cold beer. You growl at me,
"It's you who have been in the sun too long."

My family comes to visit. They enter the yard
through the gate, a stream of them
carrying casseroles, steaming pies.
As they pass him I whisper who he is.
Don't stare, I say. *You especially,* I hiss
to Aunt Helen, who does. They all do.
He sees them, lowers his limpid eyes.

I peer out the window, against the rising sun.
Gone, I think with a pang.

But I am wrong. His head lifts
from the damp grass. He has only been sleeping.

I suggest a more comfortable chair,
offer to go get a cushion.
You stalk behind him, pushing
the barrel into the small of his back.

Your voice is harsh, reminding me
you were a soldier. You show me the stash
of knives hid in the folds of his robe,
tell me the ropes look loose, I should fix them.
I avert my eyes.

"Do you find him handsome?" my mother asks,
appearing beside me.
Oh yes, I think, settling his feet
in the grass, retying the knots.
His hands lie still in his lap.

What more can I do?

Who is responsible? Who shall we call?
You raise the rifle to your shoulder,
bend to the sight,
tell me to move aside.

Barcelona, The Spanish Civil War:
Alfonso Laurencic Invents Torture by Art

Flogged by color
and its cubist cousins—not
what Klee and Kandinsky
had in mind, but war,
of course, nearly always
breeds genius.

The freakish sun
weeps through green panes
into a tiny cell
tarred inside and out
to magnify heat.
A plank-bed is angled to prevent
sleep, bricks and litter
piled to make the shortest walk
impossible.
Nowhere to look
but the curved wall—
optical illusions close enough
"to tear the victim's nerves to shreds,"
spiral him into nausea.

We know the body can be made
to lose its recollections birthed in music,
its desire for bread
and sex, its only remaining wish
confession.

Who'd have guessed how easily
the brain opens its many mouths
to red.

The sublime rides a pogo stick,
vaults beyond ridiculous, beyond
heinous—

What luck—
a prisoner could crawl into Bunuel's
giant eye torn by a razor,
disappear through that ragged hole into
the mind of the maker.

ED MADDEN

Light

Two black dogs eat something dead
in the middle of the stubbled field.

The field is empty. The dogs pause
to watch cars drive by, turn back to the dark

carcass, hidden in the stalks, last year's
harvest. The field is not empty: it is full

of light. The dogs eat what they find.
I can barely see them in the rearview mirror.

The sun spreads its cold and careless light
across the sky, the fields, the lonely road.

Story

after Eavan Boland

The only legend I have ever loved is
the story of a boy far from home, and his father

standing on the road, waiting. Neither has a name.
The boy sits in a bar in Oxford, his beer

warm. The bar is filled with men, loud
with laughter and smoke, the sweet smell of hops.

Story of exile and return—wasn't the return
always the point? And yet the courage of those

first steps away, those dark streets
beyond the bar lined with linden and plane.

In the Sunday school flannel-graphs,
see the young man among the pigs,

see the spent fortune, the frowning brother,
see the father, his always open arms—

flat figures from a cardboard box.
I have never loved that story. Once,

I was ready to make any bargain.
Once I wanted to go home, back

to what I first loved, a small house
in the bean fields, marigolds at the steps,

my father on a green tractor, plowing
the rows, bare feet on the wooden porch.

But now I know the story isn't true,
just another form of grief deferred

for a father somewhere, somewhere a son.

Cabin Near Caesar's Head

for Rod and Ed, October 2005

The moon is luminous. We sit quiet
on the back porch. To the north,
Brevard, the cabin's front yard
a valley of lights; to the south

Caesar's Head, the Devil's Kitchen—
that cold cleft in the mountain
where we'd stopped only hours before—
and the dark valleys of South Carolina.

*

The leaves aren't turning yet, the summer
too dry—only the sassafras and sumac,
gold and red, and a bruise of dogwood
at the front door. The Joe Pye weed

towers over Slick Rock Drive,
here, just off See Off Mountain Road.
A dead copperhead lies coiled in the road.
A woodpecker, tentative, tests a tree.

*

They've had the cabin for years. They tell us
stories of storms, Hurricane Ivan—
even here, so high—ripping off
the screen porch. Lightning, rattlesnakes,

a forest fire only yards away.
The eerie quiet when the valleys fill
with clouds. Quiet now, four men
talking quietly beneath the moon.

*

There's a kind of openness here—
it's not the vodka tonics or the moon—
just the way two men may be
together. They made themselves a place.

We visit the falls. Ed stops,
can't make the long walk.
Rod heads back at the first falls.
We stand in the spray, thanking them.

*

The roads are lined with sumac and aster,
the shadows filled with galax, coltsfoot,
the small flowers of the closed gentian—
lilac and white, bloom that won't open.

The guidebook says they're rare, but here
they are. Bees force their way
into the blooms. The road is dark.
The ferns turn golden in the sun.

REBECCA MCCLANAHAN

Ex-Brother-in-Law

Without the law, there is no brother,
and no ceremony to mark the breaking.
Christmas Eve from the box packed away last year
we uncover the stocking stitched with your name,
not knowing what to do with it. Later as we gather
to watch family slides projected on a sheet,
your face surfaces among ours, miraculous
as the imprints emerging on the shroud of Turin.
When you were here, how simple it seemed,
the pattern of blame and solution: If only you would turn
that way or this, if only you would disappear,
my sister's life could begin again. But what of *our* lives,
the severed sisters, aunts, brothers, nephews, nieces,
fathers, mothers—all those unregistered
couplings of hearts— left to wonder
if you were ever ours, and by what decree.

Have you married some new family, are you sharing
their holiday feast while we sit here
at the table you refinished—your windburnt hands
with the freckled knuckles, rough-hewn hands
that sanded until the grain revealed itself,
the complicated whorls beneath the surface
where so much of you remains. The daughter
you started fourteen years ago wears your face
and keeps growing. And your son still brags
about the time you accidentally shot a power-driven
nail through your hand while building
a skate ramp— *For me!* he sings proudly. *For me!*

It's the small things that make a job,
you once said as you knelt eye-level to the task:
this cabinet you built to store the mementos,
all the odd, unmatched relics that have no place.
You worked two days and we were satisfied.
No , you said, *it's the finishing that matters.*
Another day's labor found its completion:
a hand sanded notch and this perfectly engineered
sliding latch with its effortless closing and opening.

Hello Love

She has sent these words into the future
to no one in particular. I find them
in next month's calendar planted on her desk.
My niece's handwriting loops back
on itself, each vowel so womanly
in its roundness, the o's might be eggs
or breasts, or the flower of an open mouth.
She has written *love*, not *lover*,
addressing the whole world of possibility.
And no comma separates the greeting
from the greeted: It is hello love she wants.
Her father is huge in his chosen absence,
growing larger each year she waits.

Not long ago, temporarily lost
between the goodbye and hello of a man
I had loved since before she was born,
I drove my niece up a mountain. I thought
it was time she saw the view, how small
our city from this height, how the shoulders
of the most impressive hills soften
when draped with fog. *It's okay*, she said.
Don't worry, he'll be back. On the way down
an approaching truck swerved, its drunken
headlights swimming, and I slammed my arm
across her chest—a mother's gesture,
inherited and useless—as if the laws of physics
alter for those we love. No matter this time.
We escaped with our lives, all our pasts
and futures hurtling toward us. At sixteen,
my hair like hers was long and heavy,
a luxurious burden I carried for love.
And when the boy left for no reason,
I sliced off the hair and hid in my room,
a Rapunzel with no means of escape.

My father, home from Vietnam,
knocked and entered, his eyes downcast
as if he were the one responsible.
I expected to hear *We love you*,
the knot of words he kept in his throat
and untied in times like these.
Instead he gave the difficult pronoun,
claiming me as his own. My answer
was to turn and throw myself onto the bed.
In that moment I would have traded
seven fathers for the boy who was gone.
What I meant to say to my niece
as the valley beneath us dissolved in mist
was that hello almost never spells love.
There is room in the hollows of goodbye
for a full grown woman to hide.
The first man who left me was not my father.
Yet still I fall again and again in love
with the backs of men. And it will be a long time
before the face opening toward her
is more beautiful than the one turning away.

Traveling

When the Egyptians packed their dead,
the brain was first to go, pulled
with tweezers through the nose.
Then a slit in the side and the rest
poured out, the soft parts they tamped
separately into Canopic jars
or simply bandaged and stuffed back in
like giblets I rummage from the cavity
of the baking hen and present
to my cat, who slurps the juicy heart
and in this I stray one step
from the Egyptians, who kept
the heart intact for the crossing
to the land of the dead, where
it would be weighed in the balance
pan, opposite Truth which was a feather.
And any heart that tipped the scales
was eaten by Amemait the Devourer.

My husband refuses to sign the line
giving it all up. *Call it my last
selfish act,* he says, *but I'm keeping
my goddamn eyes.* I'm a card-carrying donor.
I've checked the blanks: Eyes. Kidneys.
Liver. Spleen. I'm holding off on the heart.
If I die this morning, by noon my parts
will be floating, not in Canopic urns,
but more like the Mason jars lining the cellar,
beets and cucumbers swimming in brine.

You can't take it with you, but we try,
like the old woman in the news.
It's my whole life, she cried
as the tractor ripped through her home,
shoveling tons of garbage, seven refrigerators,
clothes, rotting food three feet high.

The excavation crew wore masks
to escape the air she slept in.

My grandmother swept up after herself
leaving nothing but a line
of grandchildren and one string of advice:
*Travel light. Take only what you can't
live without.* When Grandpa died,
she had nineteen dollars. She bought
a bus ticket and packed a suitcase,
one dress for each season.
On my overseas trip, I carried
bread and cheese and one small suitcase
filled with all the wrong things,
nothing fit for the weather.
The mummy I saw was Cleopatra,
age eleven, daughter of Candace,
who took with her a wooden comb,
a string of berries, a floral leaf.
Something for vanity, something for hunger,
something for memory's sake.
When my aunt died, we picked through
the rubble. Bundles of birthday cards,
widowed buttons, scarves, napkins pressed
flat in the backs of drawers.
Finally it took a bonfire.
And the things we couldn't live without
fit easily into a hamper.

TERRI MCCORD

Metering

Jacketed in orange and hulled
in a double kayak
we beat time
on the still marsh waters
for a late-afternoon tour.
We slap thighs in synch, our hands
metronomes swatting gnats.
Our paddles break rhythm
as I try to match your course,
chopping the surface
and sending our boat
gliding sideways and slow.
We drift middle-aged and childless
in this liquid netherworld where
beauty resides in thick oyster beds
and the spits from a ragged sand bar
and the tisking ticks of dragon flies.

The native guide points
out two dolphins in our wake,
one bobbing in our path so close
we see the blowhole
and hear a snort of jest;
the guide explains that dolphins follow
heartbeats, and his wink and quip
are to the other boats.
You tilt your head to shoulder,
wiping sweat as I let my fingers scissor
like minnows in the water, then cup my hand
over a tiny wet swell. *Maybe we carry more
than we can see?* You row
us straight, the boat seeming to rise,
and I finally stop counting strokes.

Principle of Uncertainty

*"The very act of observing a phenomenon inevitably effects
that phenomenon in some way."*
—Werner Heisenberg's Relativity Principle

I am nothing lacking him.
When he is not present, I am everything.
If he walks out, I alter.
He says I am small, but as he nears,
I grow larger. I diminish
him with a look, my eyes an equal sign
at cross purposes, sum of sun
making him disappear, but I close blinds,
and I reappear undone,
gaze as he shuts the door behind both
of us really. But I finish
comparisons: his angle can not matter.
He is long gone without me,
his movement unseen, my motion for distance
withdrawn. See him as he
is, stand still, standstill, still I wish. That changes
everything. This want
to know falters, this need to remain
in the dark.

Nine Years Later I View a Painting

after Carl Haag's In der Wüste (In the Desert), *1859*
—*National Gallery*

Here, the camel lies
in the Bedouin desert,
wasted by heat and all ribs,
a staircase that goes to sky.
The watercolorist seems to say
the harsh sands hold no answers,
that conflict is bad, but still we wait
for the animal to begin breathing
and roll to his feet.

I realize I am speaking of something else.

There, she had enough x-rays
for an album and a drawer of saved
hospital bracelets to link a chain
to the sky. The two halves of her chest
seemed to open finally to let her in.
Was it exposure too?
and the breathing stopped
and the ribs settled
and she looked dead three days already.

KEN MCCULLOUGH

Diet for the Smallest Planet

Most of my life I've been eating shit—
some of it I've prepared myself,
others have contributed a goodly share
but I've always fed myself—no one's forced me.
By now I'm a shit gourmet—shit soufflé,
shit-over-easy, shit cobbler, shit on the cob,
shit kabob, shit tartare, shit purée, shit
consommé, shit à la king and a wide array
of shit sandwiches—you name it—well-presented
with all the trimmings. So now I fix it for others
so that they will consume it, too
and join me in my misery. But it
doesn't always agree with everyone—
there are those who turn their noses up
and inevitably I must dine alone.

Though We Carve Our Names in Water

Isla Contoy

1

Flights of frigates shear the air,
land and bulge their ruby throats;
palms bend the will of wind and
mangroves suck the salt from sunlight.
On the east, waves pulverize the rock
while white sand builds at the west—
the island walks to the mainland.
Nurse shark, devil fish and grouper
pay no attention just to you.

2

Never ride the tortugas, never
question the baracuda's glare.
Don't trust the residents with blades
whether cormorant or iguana.
Don't mock the manta's undulations,
or patronize the flying fish
pretending to be dolphins.
Don't think to drink up any blue.
Never darken this island.

Domestique

1.

Rising from her well-appointed desk
she slips past her napping husband
and photos of their sons, out through
irises, peonies and tidy vegetables.
She skirts the cabin and the dock
runs her hand along the warm canoe
follows the lake past the locked gate
the mailbox and down the trail to the
river which is running high. She slides
the poems from her shirt and holds them
under, watching their terrified eyes.

2.

There was a stink in the kitchen and
a small stain spread on the ceiling tiles.
In the dead of winter they'd heard churlish
clucking, desperate, between the walls.
One night he came home, and there she was
on the step ladder, with a mask on,
yellowed confetti littering the floor.
Many tiles lay broken in the mess.
He was ready to laugh when she pointed
to the decayed bodies of two squirrels
twisted together like Byzantine martyrs.

3.

He takes her from behind on her mother's
plush white carpet in the mirrored living room
of their Frank Lloyd Wright house. Her eyes
are clenched and her breasts swing back and forth.

She growls as he grasps her by the hips
their tanned bodies moving like a well-oiled
but out-of-place machine. Later, the whole
family stands around the grand piano
singing. The flocked tree is decorated
with ornaments from around the world,
the buffet laden with catered delights.

4.

He painted the room tomato bisque.
They got a dog. She tried to conceal
her visitors from him. The mirrors
of their smiles dissected each of their
respective follies. This night, decisions
are deferred to the bright courtyard
where their faces are unlined, their voices
clean: they know just where they have to go.
He slips out of his notebook. The archway
faces magnetic north. The inky order
of morning confronts her as she writes.

5.

Up a bur oak just before dawn
he turns the shotgun toward himself
clicks off the safety and forms his lips
around the muzzle. The wind stops.
Taste of oil. He palpates the trigger.
Two forms moving through the dark.
He turns the barrel toward the first
steady on its heart. Dark. Darkness.
Up in a tree, killing things. Himself.
Lowers the barrel and waits for dawn
and the red thread around everything.

RAY MCMANUS

Red Barn

I.

In the morning, before the sun
collars the trunks of large oaks,
something else rises without permission.
I squirm from it like it's
some kind of irritation—sand
in the bed, a crooked mirror on the wall—
and call it the awakening. But it's just another
affirmation of what I don't have
beside me, what I won't find in the closet,
what I can't see beyond the dust
flittering in the sunlight around
the Mason jar on the ruddy brown dresser.

II.

If I am awake, I hope that it was
just a dream, something I can cling to
when the water hits my back.
I am heavy. Under the covers
there is a way out, a possibility, a rub.
She is beautiful and soft.
I stroke and beat and press down
with my thumb to hold back the eruption,
think about beach sand in the joints, the salt
in the corners of my mouth. I take
my tongue lick the edges, see
the weeds in her hair, smell
the ocean in her skin, feel

the soft folds, the hard lines with each thrust,
the moist center... release.

It is time.

III.

There is nothing I can say
about the way things smell
on Sunday mornings: chicken
smells like chicken, fried gravy
smells like fried gravy. Perhaps
I could point out what smells
like ash and what smells like dirt,
but the lid kept tight on the pot
becomes what I hear:
a comfortable hiss, a crackle,
a pop, the absence of water
on hot steel, the small silences.

IV.

The sun shows the gaps in the planks,
makes walls look like they are closing in.
I want to run outside but I find myself
looking somewhere past the wheelbarrow,
ladder, hoes and shovels; beyond the barrels,
ropes, rakes, and chains; behind old doors,
plaster casts, sheets of glass and slate.
I find the feathers and the dark spots
in the dirt, old stories about baby chicks
pecked to death by older chickens
because of the simple specks of difference.
And then it starts. The inevitable whimper
that turns to drone, turns to rhythm,
turns to sounds I have heard

before, sounds that I never want
to hear again: dirt slung in the bottom
of a jar, a fist rubbed against the reeds,
the belt on Trudy's back. And I
know my time is going to come.
The wolves are at the door.

V.

I rub the blade against the ridges on my thumb
slow enough so that the edge catches each one.
I stop at the center, hold there, apply pressure.

Point of view is clear in the field, there is nothing
between me and the horizon, but a house, a kitchen
window. I watch the mother die. I watch the son blame
himself. I watch the father look down. There is no other
way to remember it. I can reach into my pockets,
dig for old roaches; think it is time to start tearing
the old man down, but he will still wrap the strap
tighter around his forearm, and I will flinch
the same way Trudy flinches, finger the small
welts, the thin barriers between interior
and exterior, and watch the way skin responds
to pain with fluid, the way blood strains just under
the surface to let me know it is there.

His eyes are closed. I keep the house always
to my back, the mouth of the row tight and even,
and let the blade slowly close the throat.

VI.

In the back, there is a lump.
The collapse is inevitable.
A pile will break down, decompose

like a kid's dream hid in the leaves –
give it time.
When wheat dies, it falls forward.
I am the earth. I cannot tell
the difference between hard and soft,
only constants. I dig the hole, listen
to metal slice the dirt. It is not enough.
The ground is stubborn, returns its shape,
won't bend under pressure, won't give
to weight, and the horizon is slowly moving
in. Still I dig, try not to talk about concussions,
unnecessary bruising, slicing the knuckle off
to gain a few extra inches, or the miles of rows
left unfinished.

VII.

I fill the hole, cover.
Move forward.

The rats are in the corn.
The old man is dead.

What is buried is buried.
I can go back to sleep.

Toilet

Your great mouth swung open, ready to eat,
ready to swallow gallons. You are known
beyond diagrams, penciled schematics,
and do it yourself manuals, beyond the
porcelain fixture. You have been called god,
the throne, the seat of compassion, the john.
Many kings have died on you, and you sit there
ready for more, letting everything go
to your head. But consider the rust that eats
from the inside out, the constant swirling,
the constant pulling you seem to have no control over.
Consider the mounds of ass on your shoulders,
the stains on your walls, the darkness in your throat.
Consider everything said to you is said from the gut.

Things to Tell My Son

I could tell him about men that piss
in their own yards, talk about women with no teeth,
perhaps talk to him about kissing babies,
how it's not polite to point, but he can kill
a man and get three to five in Florida.
Maybe talk to him about canter and sway,
the way balls bounce and ropes slip, sliding down
the wrong way, crawling. I could tell him
about Florida, teach him a little Spanish,
teach him a little Hemingway, talk to him
about pipe smoking and guns, explain to him
why they don't necessarily belong
together, how that's a good thing. I could tell
him about gardens full of dead pets, lugged,
dropped and covered without procession
or sermon, uprooted by too much rain,
the strain of having to recover the bone
itself, the shadows that are not his, whispers
behind hills where boys, aged twelve, are picked up,
set trashcans on fire and let them roll, limp
like cripples, like dogs shot or hit in traffic.
Or I could just shut up, let him figure it out.

MAURINE MELECK

There You Are

trying to act nonchalant
in one of your last sessions
with your analyst
because he's moving away
so you find yourself
talking about the jelly beans
in his candy dish,
the effects of rising
interest rates on the economy,
when you really want
to get down on your knees
and beg him to stay
or cry out that you'd donate
your right leg to science
for one night in his arms.
When he suddenly says,
"There's a very large bug
on your left breast."
You look down, see its thick
black body, lengthy antennae
sway like flags in the breeze.
Then he says, "Hold on,
I'll get it," but it's too late
as you're already shaking it off
and the bug jumps away
and lands on the couch.
You and your analyst examine
it closely as entomologists.
My God, it must be three inches long.
It doesn't look like a cockroach,
doubt it's a spittlebug,
not enough legs for a spider.

The doctor lifts up your personal
file—but you quickly remind him
that you are a bug lover.
Together you open
the third floor window,
scoop the bug on a piece of paper,
ease it out onto the narrow ledge,
and let go, hoping it can fly.

The Moon Has Settled

in between the slats
of my living room blinds.
Full tonight and highlighted
like important lines of a book,
if I went outside I could probably
read a romance novel under it.
But forget that.
The wind accompanying its celestial
glamour would push me back indoors
before I turn one page, unlike
those lovers in werewolf stories
who thrive on ample moons
and meowing winds where only
one sweetheart will survive.
I'll sleep better knowing
I've brought in a stray kitten,
rescued from the biting air.
Now she can purr near my side
while I read a tender fiction,
heated by a passionate sun.

SUSAN MEYERS

Someone Near Is Dying

To sit for hours by your bed
is to gaze at the day's periphery,

the chickadee at the feeder fidgeting
like a four-o'clock insomniac.

My desire is to leap into the midst
of forgetfulness, its dreamy scatter.

What does your every move show
if not, *I am still alive?*

If this moment, bare as twigs,
is the only one, let it be

the limb, in its loose skin
of lichen, tilting at clouds—

not the branch stunted
from lack of promise or light.

The beauty of Spanish moss is the curl
of its beard lifted by wind; of brown

grass, its inclination toward green;
of the chickadee, its brave opinion

of strangers. Listen, Mother—
thunder, out of season: an old woman

at the end of her day, humming.

Guitar

On any given night it picks its way
down the canyon, one step
almost in front of the other—agile enough
to slip by whatever spells trouble.
Forget fear. It slides down rocks, if it has to,
to reach bottom. By day, a red bandana
or straw hat, and why not?
No map, just crosshatch and parallel.
It inhales the heat, and the pinched cold
creeping off the mountain.
It lives alone, turns its back to the wolves.

Say it's a tin cup with bent handle.
Peyote in full bloom. A train
pulling rich cargo across the horizon.
Tequila. A thumbnail piercing the skin
of a lime, the ripe shower that follows.

Neither the Season, Nor the Place

Lake Santee, SC

Some mornings I mutter down the hallway
of our marriage and open the only available door.
But once in a while, say on a warm January morning,
I ride out with him on the smooth lake of it,
our small boat in the midst of quivering loons,
the soprano of their notes—not calls, really,
but soft barkings—reaching out into the air
like questions that reorder the day.
In these high-pitched tones of small dogs, the loons
sound wounded, but they're not:
they drift on the honey-sweet water, unfettered
and safe in their wintering. We watch one bob
and dive, and just when we're distracted, it resurfaces
a few feet from us, a white-breasted surprise.

Another and then another loon rises in place,
stretches its thick neck, flapping its wings,
and shakes off a shiver of water. They appear
and disappear. Around us their quiet yelping, the rising
and diving—our boat rocking occasionally in another
boat's wake. Their bodies glide in a slate cloak
of understatement, not the black-and-white
plumage they're known for, their bright-checkered
beauty—this being neither the season, nor the place.

RICK MULKEY

Blind-Sided

*"Only one person is known to have been hit by
a meteorite. On November 30, 1954, Mrs. E.H. Hodges
of Sylacauga, Alabama, was sitting in her house after
lunch when a 9-pound stone crashed through the roof
and hit her on the thigh."*

—Walter Sullivan, We Are Not Alone

Nine years and three days later I drop to the earth
with considerably less speed, but with as great
an impact, or at least that's how my mother tells it.
And she lived to tell about it, as did Mrs. Hodges,
once she recovered from the shock, the thrill
of coming as close to the eternal universe, eternally,
as a few inches. But isn't that always the way.
One moment we're minding our own business,
wandering about in our lives, no apparent course,
the next we're rolling diapers into a meteoric knot
and hurling them into the pail.
Or, as with my friend J., we're finishing
our lunch when out of nowhere a wife stiffens in her seat
and looks across the room. There's nothing there,
but still she looks, hoping that the words will fall
from the heavens. There is no easy way
to say it, so she leans into the table
and without apology says she's had enough,
that it's her turn to find herself, that the monotonous
orbit she's been forced into won't do. Her tight, stony fists
hang in her lap. Silences stretch light years,
and all the feeble attempts at reconciliation
will never reach her now. It's the same feeling
as when Mark Preston blind-sided me,
stone-hard knuckles snapped the ridge of my nose,

a stream of blood flared into the parking lot.
Some other kid might have swung back, but I was horrified
at the pool filling my palm. My blood,
I repeated to myself as I sat there
quietly while a friend finished off the guy I believed
was trying to finish me. He never knew what hit him.
Nor did Mrs. Hodges until they calmed her, medicated
her from a pain that wouldn't end. Years later she'd wake
to the fiery ache in her leg, a reminder of what she'd
been and what she'd become, survival's gravity
twisting her life into one deep breath, like the first breath
that coughs up the phlegm of another world and deposits
it right here in this one where all around us stars
flare into bits of battered stone, and the universe
leaves each of us alone to explode in all directions.

Insomnia

The way, from 30,000 feet, the earth
   looks like marble, or sorghum swirled
in a batter, beaten and mixed up,
   this is how it is in the beginning
of the middle of the night.
   We think we need miracles
but it doesn't have to be
   parachutes opening, or the chemistry of yeast.
Why not my life as sawdust
   layered over a concrete floor, or the muddied
light of rain puddled in a footprint,
   or an olive ground into white linen?
How can we resist waking?
   The night is a lie whispered
in our ears, the breath perfumed
   with the scent of fresh peaches
and only a hint of hurt in the hard, bitter pit,
   a dark bruise rooted in light.

Why I Believe in Angels

Because I've seen their musculature joined
hip to hip in parked cars, their bones,
under the glisten of skin, twisting into flight.
Because I've seen them rock through one another
in that oldest of nights, in that moonless hour of clarity
when the field mouse briefly turns its head from danger
and only a wingbeat marks its passing.

Because I've heard them speak in tongues
in late night bars as their bodies writhed
in the stage's strobed light. Because I've seen
their breasts encircled in the incense of cigarette,
and I've held their heart's beating planchette and deciphered
scribbled prophecies on back-alley walls and discovered
their words, like ours, are mere ticks on a clock.

Because I believe the quark and lepton that leap from lover's
        mouths
were once part of a rotting branch on Centauri Prime,
and because I wake at night full of a past compressed beside me,
the voices of friends whose wives left or husbands cheated,
who, faced with such truths, are certain they didn't know:
"I stood there," they confess, "though someone else possessed my
        body."
Then all I can imagine are the unpaid bills a life accumulates,
the voracious guilts and minor misdemeanors, the interpenetration
of morphogenetic fields that allows the rat in Seattle to convey
the way through the maze to a rat in Boston to the rat inside my
        head,
and because I can't ignore these signs, because I can't ignore,
I find, without looking or understanding, my wife's hands,
or my son's hands, crossed upon my chest,
and there like two wings they've ended their journey.

ROBERT PARHAM

When Our Men Get Together

This week the men in our family sing.
Trunks with banjos and guitars make their way
down I-95, down the Waycross two-lane,
around the beltway, both sides of Atlanta.

Once all the families were tied by kin,
by the knots that cousins and nephews made,
by the frog-filled stories gigged, the cigarettes
and liquor taken early, like sex too soon.

We're like others now, too many divorces,
ex-wives familiar faces near the campers
in the infield at Darlington, Talladega;
all the weedy paths begin to tangle.

We play golf near the mill that runs one shift,
drink beer and call home before the last one,
and hear somebody's kid rev an engine
over the rumble and thump of Blaupunkts.

But we'll sing again and the night will churn
like a bad stomach on good whiskey warmed
by Bill Monroe, and Wilbur will forget
he's dying of cancer this week, and yell

like tobacco season just rung up a good year
at the warehouse, the buyers moving along
like women in Sam's happy as June bugs
at what they see and smell; we'll beat good time

on the sound holes of our Strats while Georgia
lights up, music the only thing mercy needs
sometimes, the only real blessing on earth
worth having, one more verse for the hell of it.

Things You Can't Stop No How

"This is the way it is," she said, and with her cane
pulled back the window curtains so morning fled
inside with the two of them. "You let it in,"
he said to her. "Things you can't stop now how," she said.

A fly, outside on the sill, shivered against the old
chill while straight shooting sun warmed them like plants,
not unlike the framed plastic of Father's unpainted
greenhouse that flapped to any breeze, all dissents.

"Sometimes you slow down for a reason," he suggested.
She smiled, aware his wisdom tapped her own, the most
she could expect, a son's love, a simple gesture
more than its sum, as in music, a rest.

"This spring the grass will grow, the bushes we'll cut down,
and the neighbors will stare as though we've lost our minds.
But in June the colors will make it as though they've seen
for the first time, and the new birds have brought new sounds."

Once, when his father was alive, the boy recalled
a ballad that always followed unanchored strumming,
an off key hum, until the words tumbled out, pitch returned,
and even the short intrusions of crickets turned forlorn.

Love, the words said, always followed the wagon into town,
tied to the back like a horse who could not pull its weight,
until the rig was unhitched, the team put up, all done;
then the horse and the man rode off, all silence, all night.

His mother chose not mysteries to share but answers,
lit the day up parting curtains, always looking west
where everyday pretends to end, where the pasture
blued to fading light, to grant permission, then, to rest.

Bill of Lading

Paid up, loaded down, moving out,
to get down the road
to be paid off

Each turn-around writ
and proof by the ton
of what we're worth on the road

Turning wheel to these wheels
dear lord fortune
she's something else

if that's not enough
the golden trip will spite
the beggar of

his worthless cane
and he'll be off
with his cup all tinny

without its music
while the drums
turn and we eke

out this triply bread
and hear our brothers
through the static

of our midnight prayers
all gone breaker
in the long night

that may not love
us, even though
this late, we own her.

JIM PETERSON

Alive and Well at the Camelback Inn

1.

Climbing the steep bank
I knew that you had found it:
the matted grass and bed of ashes
surrounded by the trees that bow
like old men digging into deep pockets.
There is so much to find here
and so much space to keep it.
My father's watch
lies somewhere in those reeds
along the lake-bank, more now
to remember him by in its absence,
and your wedding band still whispers
in the ashes of some fire
now cold and green as grass, but
the gap beneath that knuckle
remains alert.

2.

It is October
and everybody comes to watch the leaves
let go as always, letting go
like the aging walker on the wire
who has known how he would die
since he was nine.
Not everyone can hold his life so neatly
like a flame in a cup of hands.
But we can know what lies
at the top of this familiar hill,

even in October
when the air is full of signs
and the wind turns back against
itself. And we can stroll
outside the inn and down the narrow path
to witness small events around the creek:
the copperhead sliding over wet stones,
the doe with head erect and nostrils flaring
before she runs, the raccoon
like a target arriving in the wake
of darkness, manipulating
with its human hands
the carcasses of mice and fish.

The Man Who Grew Silent

He had nothing more to say.
He hadn't gone to work in weeks.
His boss had let him go
After the first three days
When he wouldn't answer
Any of their questions.
But he's sure they parted as friends.

His wife took him by both shoulders
And tried to shake some sense into him.
He had not spoken to her since August
And the nights were getting cold and long.
His fingers trailed down her spine
As she turned away and left the house.
The trunk was packed already, the children
On a bus. He waved from the porch as her car
Disappeared. He turned around and smiled
Into the almost empty room, TV
With a blown tube and a blank face
Like his own, but inside, a storm of dreams
And re-runs.

It felt good to sleep until he woke
To silence in the morning, hands behind
His head deep into the pillow. He watched
The bare limbs shake in the wind outside.
He worked all day to keep everything
In its place and followed all his thoughts
And all his secret voices unwinding
From his head until the tape ran out.

He did not ignore necessities. He stood
Among the gleaming aisles of food
Reading the praises of cereal and beans.
He studied that accumulating silence
Of his friends waiting in the line to pay.

He loved his box grown overstuffed
With mail. He loved the faces of the people
He knew so well calling to him from his lawn
Or pounding on his door. One day
A van pulled up and three men
With dark glasses and a key came in.
He'd been expecting them. They led him
To the van. When he arrived someplace
The rooms were bright and large. A woman
Held his hand and looked into his eyes
But did not persist in speaking. The men
Who led him away did not speak at all.
He loved the way everybody was being
So good about it. They left him in a room
With a table, a chair, and a bed.

He lived there for a long time.
They left him alone. Each night
The lights went out, but the silence
Glowed for him even in the dark. One night
He heard the walls humming
And when they stopped to breathe
He took a breath: a long, deep drawing in
Of air that didn't end. He felt ignored
All the way through, cold from the collapse
Of his presence in the room, and found
Himself outside the wall.

The guards saw him in the yard
But couldn't stop him,
The chain link fence dividing him
Into diamonds
Drifting off in all directions
In the cold night air.

The Owning Stone

1 The Ritual

Three years ago I cleared this field
dragged the pines and sweetgums
and stacked them at the edge
home now for black widows and hog-nosed snakes
and the green-turning-to-brown chameleons
I left three great oaks and half a dozen dogwoods
scattered the bahia seed by hand and now
the grass is good enough for grazing
but there will be no horses here nor cows

from the edge of cliffs and salt water
I chose it for its size and weight
for the way it lies in the palm
for the way it both absorbs and reflects the light
but trees already know the heft of stones
hold them in their roots for a hundred years
so I throw the stone to a far corner and run
to find it burrowing under dead leaves
I throw it again to another corner and another
then into the center then out again to the edge
running to find it each time
making these trees this grass this piece of land my own

2 Voices

Last night I named the stone
when it was too tired to be thrown
and when it refused to take the light
from my lamp into its crystal striation
in the silence of these old walls the stone
reminded me of my father's sightless
eye that looked both dead and alive at once

William of the dapper wingtips
and the big plans that sometimes worked
of the two day beard on weekends
and the smell of hard sleep that lingered on his body
of the tiny voice that leaked from his bad eye
when he dozed in the summer dusk

while I lay close against him and that small
voice like the TV turned very low said
stay right where you are kid and you'll succeed
and I said *I'm going to live far away in Texas*
or Maine where the lobsters are free and the cliffs
are like castles looming over the stormy ocean
and the eye just laughed and rolled aimlessly
in my father's head

3   Mirth

I want to speak to the stone
but I know it will only listen
named for the eye of a dead man
it is a blurred face in the background of a photo
less than that
less than something lost and forgotten
nothing without me
the object of a game of solitaire
cold in my hand empty of everything
but itself and I open the door and hurl it
its flight invisible in the darkness
the tree frogs are full of mirth
the whippoorwills are voices within voices
the stone drops onto soft ground far away
and creeps under leaves

4   Choice

I can imagine the flight of anything
especially a stone named
William who was my father and who owned everything
one thousand throws of a stone in every direction
it could not hide from me in the dawn
I would take the stone back to where I found it
but the price of a ticket is high and the car is blowing smoke
I would throw it in the lake
but I know I would only follow it
and its advantages in deep water are great
no I must own up to the fact of this stone
I have chosen it and it me though it complains bitterly
it is my one simplicity my one secret
true because no one wants it
what remains of my father's land can hold it

here you can take it for a while
let it ride among your change let it ride
in your breast pocket among the points of pens
let it become lost among your papers
or under the furniture of an unused room
and I will find it some night when we
have talked ourselves into morning
as I first found it one day in July
on the coast of Maine in a small cove
where the grains of sand were stones

ELLEN RACHLIN

Crocuses

I gave my sister the perfect
perennial to place among
the cracked, unmatched
silver stones of her terrace.
The crocus seldom fails
a careless lover of gardens.

Mid-March, chilly dew smothers
mud and grasses while delicate tips
of pink, yellow, and pale purple
grandiflora burst like an argument.
For weeks they blaze
beyond their green skins:
I remain inviolate
unless crazy catches me.

Radishes in Childhood

My neighbor has no children;
she finds things to do.
No one at my house misses me.
This afternoon we plant radish seeds
between her cold-frame box
and the cellar door.
We dig up dots of earth
and crush them into powder.

Will the seeds disappear and never grow?
Seeds need rain, but I'm afraid
of rain when it rattles
my attic bedroom window
and lands just short of me.
It seems okay to do without rain,
but she explains rain matters
and how to make do
with what you have
      as you grow.

RON RASH

Shadetree

After Sunday noon-dinner
men gathered where truck or car
motor hung from an oak limb
like some trophy shot or yanked
from wood or river, and though
all had their views on just how
and what needed to be done,
not one took off his cufflinks
rolled his sleeves around biceps.
Cigarette butts and Red Man
marked an afternoon's passing
as each held his place as if
before a hearth, the log-chained
weld of steel hanging sometimes
for a month, huddled around
so it might spark and fuel
an allowance of language
beyond utility, though
always first the lexicon
of engines before slow shift
to story, joke and sometimes
the hotwired valves and pistons
making racket in the heart.

Bloodroot

Two weeks without frost, first bloom
of trout lilly and bloodroot,
sun soaking through gorge-rocks stir
the gorgon heads underneath,
unknotting, rising through veins
in granite, split tongues tasting
bright air, divining heat-spill
where outcrops angle and jut
to catch noon sun, places where
I bring snake stick, pillowcase,
work my way upridge. They pay
by the foot, those handlers who
lift the snakes on Sunday nights,
holy fools, I call them though
I was too, before four years
away at Bible College,
schooling they helped pay for so
I could better learn the Word,
learned instead the world, returned
a felled angel, my God now
a bottle of Jack Daniels
held like prayer, my service
work I find when someone needs
barbed wire strung up, sheet rock hung,
whatever else gets the bills
in Randy Davidson's hand,
liquor rising behind him
like Jacob's Ladder, the ring
of his register sweeter
than a preacher's altar call.
Serpents pay best, satinbacks
old folks call them, big ones bring
thirty dollars, so each spring
I climb this ridge, always hear
the hum of resurrection

as I near, the pillowcase
filling with a muscled flow
like water in a suckhole,
and when I've caught all I can,
take them to Reverend Holten,
who does not know I listen
beneath the window those nights
he and the congregation kneel
on concrete, pray for my lost
backslid soul in vain before
they raise their serpents and I
raise mine that it might crawl down
my throat, settle and coil,
still the rattling in my heart.

The Reaping

As supper cools, fireflies spark
dew-grass like stars on a pond
and still the hay baler hums
in the meadow, he does not
need screech owl cry or his wife's
linger by window to know
what keeps his son in the field's
gathering darkness, so steps
through barbed wire strung in April,
already sagged by fence posts
leaned like corn stalks after hail
because the boy would not
listen, would always search for
short cuts, even as a child
leaving weeds between bean rows,
cheating on nails when a shed
needed shingles, each short cut
leading toward this evening
when his father will smell blood
sizzling on belts as he frees
skin-stripped arms from the rollers,
chides his son for half a life
lost to save half a minute,
before kissing the cold brow,
forgiving what steel cannot.

ALEX RICHARDSON

A Momentary Stay

It's an unusually lazy stretch of afternoon,
In-laws out, children hiking the well-worn holiday trails
This 5th of July with Mom.

And I and the dogs listless on the dock,
The lake water rolling up,
Sopping the green backs.

I'm Hamlet in a damp bathing suit.
Read or write. Another beer? Shot of rum?
A mixed hound noses tennis balls at my feet.

I sip and listen
For the tires returning
On the gravel drive.

That's when the thing occurs that might make you think
You're reading a Frost poem—
A thick bird swerving through low branches

And out of sight. I think he must have seen me
So idle with a book and a pad before me,
Must've decided, by God, he'd make up my mind,

And do so in such a blackish blur
That I couldn't name him, couldn't,
Like a 5 year old boy with Audubon in his pocket,

Say *Hawk* or *Crow* or *Turkey*,
Could only reach for the pad and leave
The mysteries of literature for another hour.

This much I can scribble, up to the moment
Where the thing vanishes,
Just as it had happened.

This is the part
Where the reader
Will have to decide.

Hammock

I back into it like an early moon,
Each muscle lapsing into perfect atrophy;
My only way of flying, a low-country trick on physics.

Above me, wrens nest in the abandoned light fixture
Hanging from the tongue and groove.
Their flight from under the porch's eave

Is like the jetstream on channel 8.
I'm a lazy weatherman who's traded afternoon showers
For the intricate cartography of wings.

Better than the sky is how I put it
To Mr. Windchime next door, his science
For reading weather: bamboo, porcelain, pewter

All hewn into spears, stars, pelicans
Twinkling and flapping an uneven song.
I'm slowing down,

A stationary droplet suspended in the roped parallelograms,
Not even that, no rain in sight,
A guy held up by holes, by nothing,
same as constellations.

HARRIET POPHAM RIGNEY

Song

This little pool of light within the dark
suggests the world is safe, at least this desk,
this book-lined room, this screen of dead white gleam
that takes the words and makes them black.

Outside lies the late evening.
The city's glow has not yet taken over
the deep and silent sea of air
in which we swim as best we can,
marooned by flesh in this grave land.

Like phosphors, fingers mark
the small currents of the rising tide,
plucking out letters to form lines that wash
upstream into the hear,
wrack in the breathing marsh.

LEE ROBINSON

Being There

Six a.m,
I get up to pee, my feet
groping for the slippers
you gave me that first Christmas
we were married—
moccasins lined with sheepskin,
half a size too small
but stretched now
to the shape of my toes.

I move in the dark
across the old pine floor
as if on ice, careful
not to wake you.
Hands held out
for furniture, I find
the bathroom, feel
the bottom of the toilet
bump against my feet,
turn to sit, then fall
with all my freight
(half middle-age, half sleep)
into the pit you made
when you left the seat up.

I confess I cursed you,
your small sin looming large
as I wallowed in the dark,
in the cold shock
of the unexpected,
and would have said something

this morning, something
about thoughtlessness,
had I not stopped at the window
on my way back to bed
and seen there, in the moonlight,
the doe, alone.

She saw me, too,
or sensed the shape of danger
near her. For a moment
we both froze
before she raised the white flag
of her tail and disappeared.
I crawled in beside you
and sent up a kind of prayer
in praise of your steady snore,
your being there.

Silk

Imagine
you are in another country,
your guidebook
to this village
years out of date.
Streets teem
with people in dusty caftans,
their faces half-hidden,
their eyes
never quite meeting yours.
You stumble on the market and ask
about the merchant who sells silk
but you get a blank look,
and when you ask again,
a sharp *No English!*

Didn't the innkeeper say
the silk was here,
or was that another town?
You bump against bodies
going the other way, bodies smelling
of sweat and spices, you come
full circle in the labyrinth
of stalls: strange fruits, birds and bats
in cages, a hundred bolts of cloth
but no silk, no silk.

Ignore the hands reaching out
with their cheap, rough goods.
Ignore the shouting, the pushing.
You will make it to the other end of town.
There you'll find a bench beside the lake
where sailboats float like butterflies.

Wait there.
Someone will come
who speaks your language,
whose little boat
takes you out to open water,
out where the village disappears
and there is nothing but the sea
and the two of you
behind the scarlet spinnaker,
the sail full of wind
and shimmering in the sun
like—yes—
like silk.

JEAN-MARK SENS

Star Pointer

Perhaps the only absolute remembrance
in the dark of my father's darkness
were the walks we took on country cinder roads.
Dust shadowed his shoes in the swash of each step
as night became more resolute
isolating the mind, curving its dome over summer fields.
The smoldering Bessemers and heaped slag
glowed under the caul of the sky's parabola.

A mile or two off the village,
streetlights and TVs' anesthetic blueness
no longer ate up the stars.
Pretending to reckon what his hand would trace
I listened to mythic names
incomprehensible pinpoints joining constellations
directions of second sight's instinct.
A desert traveller's knowledge, helmsman's clear eye,
celestial guide of the obscure where the path brightens:
pilot, killer angel of hot cerulean sky
guiding his crew the way back home
after having released the overweight of metal
crashing more metal, turning stones into dust
implosions leaving dead men intact
bleeding deep their innards.

Orion's shield, the Great Bear Arcturus revealed
the lucky tail of Cassiopeia, his tongue
articulated maps, passages between
searchlights and flack.
In the storm blanking all expression,
signals sizzled on the radio,
and then, with a pull of his neck,

his head loomed over closer constellations
as the plane freed through a growing dawn
climbing higher toward familiar lands.

Bloom

Seeds started weeks ago over a wet cotton ball
housed in a glass jar.
The envelope peeled to the fat of the grain,
shape of a green comma
forcing its head through a dangling caul—
no spectacular birth here,
a parturient slowness unfolding what is given in the seed.

Bearded filaments web small roots
already grasping, pushing forth small stanchions,
chrysalide's travail building slowly
a stair-shaped leafage unwinding step after step
like the DNA assemblage in a school science lab,
the Great Carpenter's work, tongued
and grooved, amino acids of brailled inevitability.

So many seeds you started,
nature dividing success from failure.
Some with a dead mechanism
never found the call of light or water
shriveled in the glass to lump peas,
others soon craned out their green heads.
Follicles gone and cotyledons grown,
you bedded the homunculi roots deep a good half inch in soft loam.

Today returning from a month long trip,
Surprise! How chance took its course in turns and dowturns
through intricacies of bushes, wind, rainwater, and sun.
Small umbel calyxes breathe in early sun
shadowing whiteness inside deep purple skirts,
later under the noon's full sight,
morning glory digitalis close, furl in.

WARREN SLESINGER

The Ring of Dancers

It was a land in league with its own remoteness;
a land half-sea; the sea, half-ledge
on a course that he had chosen when he crossed
over a thousand mapped square miles of openness:
water and wind that carried the clouds toward an island
so far north of the norm that it was known
by its coordinates instead of a name for what he wanted:
a world in reach of his rigging.

Instead of spillways, a place with hills where the pines
stood still. On the porch that overlooked the harbor,
he could light his pipe and rock as slowly as the boat
that rode below him on the ripples of his own reflection.

He watched a wave lift and pound itself to spray.
Where in the world with its gulls and its garbage was the shore?
It was not on the horizon that dipped and drew the eye
that watched the whitecaps and the sky into a network of wrinkles
while the map was flapping in his hand, and he tried to locate
this windspit of sand, this island in the North Atlantic
that traded with the traffic of the screeching birds.

He let go of the wheel, and the sea steered him
over the lifting swell toward the clanging dome of the bell buoy
that rolled above and below him with one cold stroke
of the tide, and the coastline came through the mist
crumbling from its cliffs.

At the landing, his sea-legs sagged.
The wake of everywhere that he had been caught up with him
in plunging undulations that washed and washed among the piling
as if the sea could not come clean of something.

It was a large world in a small place.
A church pointed a wooden steeple at the sky above a cluster
of clapboard houses. The women knotted their kerchiefs,
the men pulled at their caps. It was bright enough to see a bead
of pinesap in a board, and the sand in the street
was as clean and coarse as salt, but he smelled the odor of fish
from the barrels in a wagon to the nets on the dock,
to the flies in the toilet where the urine spattered in the stall.
Outside, he saw a fisherman pluck his pipe
from his mouth, and spit in the wind for luck.

In a store, he bought a postcard and a sweater
at a bargain table from a blue-eyed blond with braids
and a smile as wide as the rippling tide.
He wanted to nibble at her neck while white bites
when she explained the rate of exchange,
but he could tell that he would lose the money
because the bell in the back of the door
clattered and clanged like a piece of loose change.

He inquired about a sign that he had seen of people
dancing in a ring, and she replied that it signified their life
together on the island. It was the folkdance of the fishermen.
They performed it once a week, just to keep the tourists
from leaving. Indeed, he had seen it stamped in purple
on his passport and the price tags in the store.
It appeared on dinner plates with epigrams and the borders
of bedspreads, tablecloths and napkins. It was in the knit
of winter mittens and matching caps. The figures of the dancers
were as tightly woven as the social order.

Outside, the sun was setting in the pines. He shivered
in his sweater that unraveled as he walked away.
On a stony outcrop where the goats grazed,
he watched a wave that summed itself up to nothing
as it crested and collapsed. Where in the world
with its knives and its nets was the haul?

At a tavern on a distant strand, the dark of the carpet
came to his knees. The women whispered;
the men puffed on their pipes and watched him
while he ate the local dish. He gave a great red gasp
when he drank the wine that stripped the lining from his throat,
and heard them joke about the time of the tide
and the feeding depth of fish.

In the window was a world that tipped and spilled.
The moon appeared too near and bright as a bulb
lit by a chain in a room too small to hold all the people
who nudged him toward the middle of the ring
where the blonde slipped her hand into his and kissed him
with her lips wet and her earrings jingling.

He stiffened at the rigid fiddling; he trembled on the trill
of the tinny whistle until the drumbeat struck him dumb.
He staggered, the line sagged; the moon rolled over his shoulder,
and the hands of the dancers caught him
when he came to the surface of the roundabout world.

Fog

We live alone, our children grown beyond the range
of our foreboding in a house that overlooks the ocean,
and watch the waves on the rocks that foam and plunge
below them as though we saw a menace in the making,

and though wrong to carry it too far, apprehension is akin
to air that swirls, thickens and surges inland from the shore:
cold and damp with a soul-dissolving odor when the tide is out,
the wind building waves somewhere else, and not knowing

is like the fog that surrounds the house and settles in the yard.
Nothing emerges from it; not the fence, the swing-set or the faces
of the twins when they were really children—just the pallor

of the youngest son who seemed to slip away from us like a ghost
through a wall and with nothing to prevent him from taking chances.
So we are left with the seen and unseen influence of the weather;
the muffled sound of the ocean, and the presence of the rocks.

Never Simple or Still

Save for the shorebirds, the beach is empty,
the barren sandbars cold, and the sea in the offing,
the sea that shimmers in the light from a high overcast,
a wind-blown patch of foam.

The man would not be on the beach
but for the blaze of memory, and the distance
of his walk is not of interest unless it reminds him
of a place like this, and it is still visible

in his consciousness: the figure of a girl
in a skin-tight suit with slipped straps; his fingers
slick with lotion; its sweet-tipped scent in the sunshine
that remains within the reach and retreat of his memory

and the interplay of wind, clouds, and light,
on the sea that is never simple or still, but the way,
his way, is always the same, and she not sharply defined;
her hair a blur, her face plain, her eyes straining to find

if he meant to quit and leave her entirely,
and yet, he remembers her little body chilly with sweat
at the end of sex when the swirling water forms a trough
that drains the colors from the shells as the tide ebbs

from the creeks and oyster beds that seem to shudder
in the surge, and slide forward in the lull; the sea
to withhold, and hurl itself at the shore again,
and his remorse has no resolution.

BRIAN SLUSHER

The Drunken Couple

God! Here they come, arm in arm,
weaving slightly as they walk,
talking loudly, looking warm,
insulated from the shock

of neighbors staring as they pass.
Each onlooker tsks regret,
whispers to a sober spouse,
"How can they go on like that?"

She holds her highball even
adjusting to his dips and jerks
and though he seems a burden
she won't let go for all she's worth.

And on their leashed dog drags them
as they share a common glass
which must one day fall broken
(at least that's what the gossips guess).

Yet nights we hear them laughing
candle-lit in their backyard
and sometimes full-out singing
—what is that tune? We listen hard.

Stand

The *Sorry* is
loud, even from across the two-lane and
through his stand of trees.
He hears the horse-laughs and ringing ice.
His wife says *Soiree*, but to him it's *Sorry*
you ain't wanted here, *Sorry* you ain't
got a polished car, too bad our people
ate your people, chewing away their place
on the land and swallowing the deeds with
each new drought.
As the gentry
nibble shrimp on the columned porch, they decide
who gets the contract to widen this route,
how much the poor ain't going to get,
who rides, who walks, then wash it down
with foreign beer and backslap by the
newly posted pond his grandma
used to fish.
So he invites
himself, wearing hunter's camouflage, to climb
into a roadside tree and sit invisible,
sighting their high jinks
through his old rifle's scope,
leading them as they sashay to the hired bar,
and he can't always quite recall
if he snapped the safety on before
he shouldered his grandpa's stock.

CHARLENE SPEAREN

Portals

And so it was. The door
appeared like a dream.
Soft, fluid, pencil-sketch
curves, an elongated
tiara carved into its center—
nothing hard like wrath,
judgment, petrified wood,
or a fire and brimstone Sunday
sermon. A call like vocation
beckoned: "Touch it."
The two hinges glistened
like a line from a poem.
I heard a gentle thud, a door
closing, tasted a sacred
space, a room filled
with the holy smell
of candles burning—
the moment
      of personal
            confession.

Her Muteness Grew Louder and Louder

"And I am somebody eating vichysoisse soup,
Vichysoisse! Oh my gosh!"
                              —Cindy Nord, The Nickel Run

The events finally bucked, then threw her high;
and as she fell like a fast setting west sun,
she sketched her ragged life. Childhood days
are collected not discarded. The journey

see-sawed between honey and pain, then settled
like silence. Alone, she stood witness to the mother's
click and clack, the father's squawk and squirm,
the cycle of living and wanting to die. Then

spiraling toward the cries, call it destiny
or coincidence, she passed a golden image,
a swooning dove. Its breast, white as innocence,
begged her to take handfuls of blazing colors:

blue, lipstick red, three shades of green. Imagine,
God knows how she painted her way past the bad-girl
feelings, past the incapacity to understand *why*.
And after a hundred fractured drawings, the high

and low notes of a thousand songs, she moved
toward the twisted reasoning realizing she would
survive. Then ascending like grace, her invitation
went out with never-ending, giving hands to those

sister-children covered with oozing questions; she
would teach each one the feathering, healing,
brush strokes, create a nurturing place, tell all who
would listen: *You can't ignore things like this.*

Tree Climber

Odd, how like the poet who desires
to hide inside her words, this limbo

child hides behind the half-draped
towel her budding breasts. Supple,

fleshy mounds suddenly drumming
for another's touch or tug. Yesterday,

she climbed a knobby buck-eye tree;
its fruit hanging like clutched fists

or stored thoughts shook as her girl-boy
body moved toward her favorite branch.

From this jaded tucked-away perch,
she watched two lovers appear then

dip their naked bodies inside the creek's
thick black water. Antoinette tasted

each pecked kiss. She almost hollered
across the whispering wind: *Bonjour!*

The greeting-call stuck in her throat
dangled like a mother wren's early

morning worm. You have seen this girl
or someone like her many times—

one who waits half-grown for five
or ten years then appears all coppered

and shiny. She wakes full-breasted,
and in a single moment appears singing
like the spring's first back-door bird.

LAURA STAMPS

Eight Zonal Geraniums

These coral and cranberry geraniums
never whine at sunrise about butterflies
resting on their laps or beetles or gnats,
and the green pages of their leaves
aren't looped with depression or an
unusual attraction to sadness. They
even seem grateful to watch the garden
through the heavy lids of petalled eyes,
to flex ruffled wrists at the clouds, and
wiggle pale ankles in moist soil, rejoicing
in another day free from destruction or
terminal disease. And every evening,
while I'm tucked away within sleep's
velvet purse, I'm sure a deer from the
forest might witness the slight bowing
of eight sturdy stems, laced only with
thoughts of good fortune and life's
blessings. Looking out the window
this morning at the blush of their
freckled faces, I bend in awe at the
turquoise tile of the sky, at dragonflies
spinning like wind chimes, at how
much there is to unlearn in this world.

Six Kittens and a Butterfly

Four o'clock in the afternoon,
second week of September,
leaves drifting from the maple
as if they were crimson ships
navigating a fall breeze, the only
evidence of Hurricane Ophelia
crawling up the Carolina coast.
Six kittens doze on the floor
among leaf-litter, their coats
swilling the last drips of sunshine,
while a black butterfly, trimmed
with scalloped wings, steps
along the lip of an empty bowl.
No worries or stress plaguing
this porch today, just the sun,
a whorl of autumn leaves, a
butterfly, and six stray kittens
snoring in bliss, unaware of the
gorgeous visitor they missed.

DAVID STARKEY

The Argument

Every Sunday in the same park
in the same small Southern town,
as seasons pass, we argue.

Dogwoods bloom white
as laundry: "Your petty,
arcane drivel." Azaleas pink
as face powder—"Trivial
way to waste a wasted life."

All through scalding summer,
the grass brown, the soft nests
of fire ants piling higher
and higher like ziggurats
to some dead god, we sneer:
"Picayune accomplishments."
"Paltry intellect."

By autumn one would expect
homicide or at least conversion
to the local Baptist Church,
but there we are to watch
the tupelo leaves turn gold
and drop, bickering about
our relative hollowness
as the turkey oaks flame red
and hickories fade
a mellow sunset blush.

Winter is worst, and best also,
I suppose. The birch trees bare,
the tiny creek sheeted over
with thin ice. Each slash
feels harsher in the cold.
The geese sound suicidal
up there above the fog.
Yet it's comforting to know
there will be no forfeiture,
though the whole world chills
and bursts like frozen pipes.

Who's worth a cipher?
Who's less than double naught?
The argument has lasted years.
Both of us are winning.

Try a Little Tenderness

–after Otis Redding

The only soul music for a thousand miles
comes from a dark room in the President
Rahkmonov Hotel. The solitary
scratch and hiss of a phonograph record—
post-millennium, who expects that noise?
In these new, doomed empires, livelihoods
depend on fresh high-tech chicanery,
the easy swindle, the obvious greed.
Tajik children starve as his voice utters
their pain. A bomb goes off a block away.
The needle lifts, returns. Smell of offal
and cooking fires, diesel exhaust, desert
mountain wind. Two guerillas listen close,
misunderstand. The evening call to prayer.

SUSAN FINCH STEVENS

Great Blues

You laugh at the water's edge
When I descend like some wild
Wind-flapped umbrella,
Wings spread eagle,
Skinny legs hanging down.
You laugh at my somber color,
My lack of song.
You laugh when I stand stock still
For what seems hours,
And you laugh when I begin to move
At the speed of sloth on Tinkertoy legs.
And when I miss my prey,
You laugh and laugh. You laugh
But do not know what I know:
That life immeasurable continues
Beneath the water's skin.
And this, too, I know: Your laugh will die,
And you will hear the last laugh
Rustling in my wings
As you wade on through gravity,
And I lift into the wild great blue.

Fireflies

Lightening bugs, we always called them,
In my childhood, in my neck of the woods.
But now we speak of fireflies
And watch the old familiar sparks
Flit and burn and die like rogue embers
Only to rise or dip and burn again,
Always again, each tiny tireless Phoenix.
How dull the jewel's of Orion's belt
In that weary plod across night skies.
No such rutted course for bright lanterned bugs
In their wild and fickle constellations.
Winged hordes dance and romp to unheard beats
And honor the quiet night with silent fireworks
That ignite the darkness hung above the two of us,
Grounded here in our own old familiar sparks,
On this hot June night when bodies burn,
And fire flies.

DENNIS WARD STILES

Mother

Mother, these last months
refuses to remember
that I am sixty-two
ten times a grandfather
and fond of bourbon
in a tall glass
that I piss
and no longer tinkle
that I am wise as a river
schooled by granite and mud.

She calls me a good boy
and believes it, sends me out
again for rhubarb and carrots.
What a bunny I become
waiting in the check-out line
with my cart full of vegetables
and my eye alert for young wives
who might be on the make.
She has no idea
of the vanity and raunch
that spice my favorite soups.

At home, the place
I thought I'd left
forty years ago
she wakes early and waits
in ambush with a hundred questions
about my life, repeating each at least
a dozen times, not really hearing any

of the answers, her eyes hooded
her innocence so deep

that the sound of my voice
as I taunt and lie
is half lullaby, half love song.

Salsa

At the downtown Acme Bar
bottles gleam and coins glint
in soft, dusty light that lets the mirror
ignore my age. There's beer smell
in the air. There's a crowd. I love these
dozens of lives
with nowhere better to be.

I'm the oldest man here.
I should go home
hum to my books
and hug my wife

but the Golden Bees
are in good form tonight.

A girl with a tumble of hair
as dark and wild as her eyes
grabs my hand
and for the third time
we salsa.

The rhythm is relentless.
Time shatters in the strobe lights.
We push off the back of the music
and dryfuck the Seventh Commandment.

Castrati

Timing was important.
We had to pick a window
when the pigs were strong enough
to survive, but not so strong
that they could break my hold
or cause real hurt.

I wasn't always easy
to sort the males and females
just an extra bulge beneath the tail
where testicles lay hidden.

As they were caught
I flipped them upside down
held their legs spreadeagled
on a waist-high wooden plank
and pinned them with an elbow.

My father was the surgeon, working
with a simple razor blade
and practiced eye. He was quick
to slice the scrotum skin, ease
out each nut, stretch its cord and cut.

If I could keep them still
it took less than a minute.
The smell was rank, a sexual brine
worse than warm urine or sour milk.

Most fought, with sharp hooves
and squeals of terror, while dust
rose from the bedding underfoot
and glistened in the sunbeams
like a blessing from the earth.

Let go, each victim
of the sacrifice would stumble
to a corner of the pen
its monologue of grunts
a meditation on surprise
and pain, with no great show
of loss, no hint of song, nothing
one long night's sleep
and a bellyful of slop wouldn't heal.

SHEILA TOMBE

Learning to Let Go

for David C. Miller, who took too much care to harm none.

Every morning, same ordeal:
without my glasses, I forget to check
for bugs in the bath;
turning on the water only to find
churning black bits of squirming torso
or wobbling antennae
swirling in the suds.

I scoop and swear and shake them
to the floor, hoping the towel there
will dry their struggling,
ease their writhing, restoring them
to scuttle or scarper;
more often than not I fail.

Again and again I have let life slip,
have not been quick enough
have not held gently enough
have squashed or extinguished
where I meant to do no harm.

I hold life, yet every day
I stumble into death. I open my house,
let spiders weave and beetles bustle,
yet by this very welcome seal their ends.

Too conscious of this cruelty
I stand helpless—
          a few twitch back into motion,
most lie, witness to my mute cry,
          letting life slip by.

Borges on the Internet

I have walked miles in my mind to reach this source,
tapping my cane against the curb of the imagination,
pacing the unforeseen as it unravels below me;

lingering by remembered shelves, fingering the words
as they collapse in chaos, letters tumbling into disorder;
each space, each byte of nothing becomes full

of this capacity to pattern into sense; shake them
like dice and they will spell the name of God,
cradle them in your hands, mold them in designs

that mirror pieces of the whole, the entire, all
of it together at the touch of the keys, an unabridged
forever in the tiger light, insistent with its cold desire

to encompass every sign, every mark from every text
in every labyrinth that ever breathed air and meaning
into the lexicon of this sightless rattle in the void

DENO TRAKAS

Zelda

On a strip of beach,
in a pink slip of sunset,
after a swim she stitched on the gulf,
she lies in sand and lets
go.

Her eyes hurt, her neck itches.
Flat people drift by, their fish eyes
swivel on her, wide open mouths.
Sea foam scrawls a cursive message
but the sand blots it.

If only she could stop the music,
Chopin, turning in her stomach,
and cut the daisy sun.
She'd swim to Mexico if he'd let her.
She gets up to hunt for shells:

no whole conch, star fish, sand dollar. . .
just scattered brittle litter,
gray, white, rust, seaweed green,
a jelly fish belly flopped,
a shifting lot of raucous gulls.

He's somewhere, watching like a general,
but he won't help or care—
she's begged him, but he drinks gin all day
and sleeps all night while they do dark
sexual things to her.

She wades into the water to rinse
the sand, the salt, the eczema,
the pigment of her skin—the veins,
the map of blood—she has opened it—
and would again—if only she could read it.

The Smaller House

We've moved into a smaller house,
mother, father, daughter, son and dog,
far from convenience but close
to claustrophobia, a "fixer upper,"
a fixated dump whose sewer line clogs.

In the masterless bedroom, too small
for a king, my wife hammers
nails like migraines into the wall,
then hangs our children on hooks,
and when the phone screams, shivers.

Her mother wants to see our little nook,
she'll bring a plant, she'll help us clean
and Martha Stewart our squalor—
she'll even cook.
My daughter, convicted to unpacking dishes,
squashes roaches to Rage Against the Machine.

My son flings his things and sonofabitches
his sorryass father, downsized again.
He hurls his own hard rock and wishes
he could split this crib, this shitshack,
this hell where death begins.

After Reading Your Dead Father Poems

for JL

I ask if I can meet your dead father.
You hesitate, say Nobody sees him but me,
but then, of course, you invite me over.

When I pull up to your house on McDowell Street,
you're sitting on the porch,
holding a glass of strawberry tea.

How does this work, I ask.
He's right there, you say, pointing to the rocker.
Pleased to meet you, Mr. Lane.

He wants to know if you want a beer.
No thanks, tea will be fine,
and you go inside, leaving me with your dead father.

I try to imagine him sitting there, but I've only seen one photo,
from the war, before he married your mama—he was younger
than we are now—we're the age he died

(of heart trouble, you used to say, before you could say suicide)
and I imagine him one of us, a high school friend who's been away
and wants to know whatever happened to what's-her-name.

I want to ask What brings you to the neighborhood?
or Have you seen my father? and How's he doing?
but I feel like a fool now that I'm here.

John's told me a lot about you, I say. He and I are buddies,
we both like cheeseburgers with slaw, basketball, tennis,
poetry—we're both democrats—I imagine him smiling as I ramble—

and both of us have lost our fathers, though mine's been gone
only two years and, well, you've come back.
I'm jealous, I say, I miss my father.

You return, hand me my tea. Y'all having a nice chat?
Yeah, but a bit one-sided, I say. I told him I'm jealous,
you have your father back.

He's a pain in the ass, always after me to change my oil
or throw out store-bought eggs, always smoking those damn Camels.
But he has a knack for ratchets, I'll give him that.

How did you come back, and why? I finally ask.
Yeah, you say, that's a good question.
I watch you listen and await your translation:

He says there's things I need to know, especially now I'm his age
and don't have a son—a man needs a son—
he wanted to tell me that.

You've got it backward, you say to him,
a son needs a father.
And even I can hear his answer: Here I am.

RYAN G. VAN CLEAVE

Approaching Thunderstorm, 1859

For Robert Creeley

by Martin Johnson Heade (1819-1904)
Oil on canvas; 28 x 44 in. (71.1 x 111.8)

Narragansett Bay
has never looked
so black, thinks
the father hunched
beside a stray dog
on the washed-up
      driftwood.
He finds a grim self-
satisfaction in
the convulsive
darkening of sky,
as if life itself might
forever remain entirely
      without color.
The pair of boats
blurring the water
will capsize in the
coming blusters
and the fools inside
will drown, he
imagines, his eyes
      aching.
How heavy the
whole world is
with everything
put in its place.
How heavy the
whole world is
when everything
      is not.

The Kudzu Queen

It's hard enough being
the woman from a small town
that nobody wants to sleep with,
but lately she has begun
to cultivate kudzu, clipping
it from neighboring oaks
and fenceposts to populate
her yard, the rows of clay pits
that line her house three deep.
In a silk ruby housecoat
and kudzu-woven sandals,
she snips strands of vine
to weave holiday baskets
for the single men in town,
collects the buds for kudzu
blossom jelly, muted green
magic that she spreads on
her belly to counteract
the parrot's-cloth of silence
her life has unwittingly become.
As her kitchen radio tinnily
sounds the swish of a jazz drum—
early Miles Davis or Satchmo
perhaps—she stretched thin sheets
of pulp across the picnic table
to dry in the sun. Car engines
whine over I-85 like summer
cicadas, but she works alone,
unseen, wishing she could
walk out of her own life
and the climb the WBEZ tower,
winding higher a foot by night
until the cool evening air is upon
her green face, and the alder
shadows are a world away.

Dear Leonard Cohen, or There Is No Music Stranger than This

I'm talking about war,
dear Leonard, the chew-
you-up catastrophe
invading the coasts
of your homeland.
The sea might wear away
at lighthouses and bother
cormorants nailed
to black rocks, but
from the sky falls
a three-ton bomb—
smooth, very smooth,
like a robin's egg.
A watch hand on a
shepherd's daughter's
wrist cuts away the seconds
while the whistling
gets louder, until
the moment where
all sound is released.
It starts with a fat
plopping, as a wet
grape makes when burst
between fingers. Then
shadows erupt and fill
the earth—think black
odors and maleficent steam
as Charon rises from blue
salt-cellars, oar in hand,
waiting to bed every
body gone slack—
and a gaping hemisphere
in unleashed. Think
thunderclaps like
barrels dropped from

a watertower. Think
warning horns blowing
in the distance. Think
lightning flashes and
hell-roar, the song of
so many bodies forever
at rest.

CEILLE BAIRD WELCH

Commitment

for Jim

Beneath the pale hot sky of August
And chanting some sweet lyric born of childhood,
We raked with drawing sticks against the ground,
Etching a house with many rooms,
Like dreams.

The loosened earth we cupped with circling hands,
And set our brows to weep into mounds,
Molding up stones of earnest sweat and dust
As porous/strong as love is
And as dreams.

We bore each stone to heap upon the next
And clung to one another in the chaff.
We pieced together scraps of hurried days,
Wrenching yarn
From the hairs of our heads.

On dark/bright scraps we laid our babies down
And swaddled them with flowers and with beads,
Holding back the rain.
And when the rain became too much determined
We dared at first to dream up other dreams,

Then went to work with mouths of twigs and moss,
Weaving with mouths like wrens do after storms.
And we, who had forgot the songs of childhood,
Heard then the August rhythms
Of our children,

And recognized their music,
And offered them our dream-sticks,
And watched our children drawing in the dust—
Houses with many rooms.

We watch our children sweat and pluck their heads.

Death of a Nightwalker

He has this thing about walking at night
alongside the highway, like now, in rain,
has this thing about possessing it all—
night, highway, rain, ditches—
this thing of possessing the whole shut world,
taking it in without interference,
and no other one in the foreground
spoiling his view of
himself.

He answers to no one in night-rain,
can be his own man in a world shut-down,
have it his way,
play around with his take on things,
and try everything on for size—
changed ambitions, or other intentions,
garments cast off by a drifter—
while he litters the sedge-grass with stuff of his wallet
and crams his good shoes in a

He can put his foot down in night-rain and ditch-mud
and ignore all the too-certain cadence of things—
road-signs, and fence-posts,
and insects rubbing against themselves,
and shadows that chew in their sleep—
can crow in the middle of the road,
if he wants to,
can dance and force the rhythm out,
pin-wheeling his arms like a mad-man
to keep from falling down;
can take the measure out of everything,
if he wants to,
and measure up to nothing, measure up to nothing at all—
not clocks, or cell-phones, or date-books or pagers,
or beasts masquerading as women,

reproaching in lipstick and blood,
telling him he does not own the world,
and will not ever,
so he might as well hang it up,
might as well hang up this walking at night,
or it will be the death of him.
Yet.

A moon is becoming where no moon should be,
becoming from distance with road-waving light:
the low light up-falling into his eye,
his left eye, just that one, his northern-most,
where no light should fall,
and he, of abandon and night and unmaking,
is not oppressed by it, but is confirmed,
and when he turns, wholly,
when he fills his other eye with moon,
it is a glad and measureless turning,
one without margin or form,
the way he might turn in a dream of dancing in ocean,
to make perfect bond with this crowed-up moon,
a moon begetting,
becoming two moons where none should become,
ripened and Saturn-ringed,
becoming beast's eyes where none should
ever
become,
and bearing down,
bearing down.

MARJORY WENTWORTH

Homecoming

If sleep has a smell, it grows here
when flowers raise their heads in the mist
to eat the light pulsing at the edge of the sky
where tapered tails of wind unwind
like roots stumbling through darkness.

After green silence of dreams
I rise and drink the warm rain failing,
dig two holes in the ground
to plant my tired feet,
because I need to live for awhile

in the black bed of earth. On this island
rolling beneath unfurled tongues of fog,
where the scent of wet salt can turn the air
to bread in my mouth, or blanch
the dark fisted vines that never wither.

All winter, jessamine and honeysuckle
holding petals in their closed mouths,
were waiting for desire
to open them, in the wind,
to lose themselves in rain.

When he Is gone my heart rearranges
within my body, where nothing seems
to move for weeks or months. Alone
I wait for his scent to return
to the empty pillow beside me.

I am like the morning glory
embedded on our fence slats,
collapsing her purple flowers
that will resurrect and inflate
with mouthfuls of air.

The smell of grass releasing
after hours of warm rain
enters the open windows of our house.
Odors move from room to room like music.
My husband listens in his sleep.

On a couch in the living room, he listens.
With children curling like kittens around his feet,
he sleeps. Beneath pages of the Sunday paper,
cradled by all that is familiar, he sleeps.
Knowing the color of love, he sleeps.

The Last Night

Drinking pints of lager and lime
like any other night, we talk
until the cigarette butts overflow
spreading ashes in the darkness.
Beneath the table, your prayer
beads click unconsciously
as the chiming church bells.
The beads shine your palm
like little black eyes. Five pairs

stare from the family photograph
taped above your cot. Posing
on a beach in Tripoli,
they watch as we undress.
Rigid, distant, and forever wounded,
your father stands in the center
like a soldier with his troops.
Nadia smiles. She is too young
to remember her banished brother.
Your mother holds a shell to her ear
and listens as if it is your voice
echoing across the Mediterranean. The shell
is dark, smooth and cut
open to the forces of the sea.

Your body still trembles, remembering
your mother's hand as it pressed
your face through the prison gates
to memorize it. The last night
your eyes search my body
as if it is unfamiliar.
We speak the wordless language
in your unheated room above
the blue and orange runway lights
where you whisper my name in Arabic
when your mind loves with your body.

I run a toenail along your arch.
Falaqua, you finally told me,
is a beating on the soles
of the feet. A punishment.
Fingering lines of the whip on your back
I feel the pain.
Scars are your body's language.
Tonight, I cannot touch you without crying.
While you sleep, I lie still,
watch the sky turning to ash,
tighten my fists around the leather
string of black beaded faith,
and I pray to my God to understand you.

To wake you, I touch
my lips to your forehead
as though you were a baby.
When you open your eyes, light
falls into my powerless hands.
And I take it.

DANA WILDSMITH

Cautionary

Mama called to ask if smoke alarms give death cries.
Hers just now squealed, she said,
and then fell to the floor.
Yes, as I've been trying to warn her,
there can be a high rate of failure-to-thrive
among smoke alarms, chairs, pencils,
and such household plunder, which is,
after all, an assemblage of orphans.
Attention is the key to prevention:
rotate your dishes
that the back bowls not feel neglected.
Turn ceiling fans off; allow them to steady themselves.
When a pen dries up, don't let
the other pens watch you throw it away.
Smooth your sheets; unbend page corners;
straighten charleyhorsed rug fringe.
Thank your mailbox for its daily gifts.
At night when you lock your doors,
say a small benediction of tumbler and wood.
Impress your pillow
with useful dreams.

Ambiance

—an open letter to the residents of Arden Meadows

We hate the lights you bring; we don't hate you.
We feared you might be loud, but you're not.
We wondered if you'd care to sit and watch
our deer graze past your decks at dusk. You do.
You could extend your fences half a foot
into our woods and we'd not notice it—
you haven't. On the whole, we'd tell you that
as neighbors go, we've no objections to you.

But once our woods and fields held nights as black
as any depths you've known, such deep sea dark
we slept in endlessness defined by stars,

until your street lamps came and hung their sacks
of hazy light to spill into our dark
and herald the extinction of our stars.

Bones

We walk our dogs through woods still winter-bare
except where dogwoods blaze as white as bone
among old pines and water oaks. This soon
in Spring our hill still hums its hymn of sleep,

a dense and dampish lullaby to green,
a tune we can't exactly hear, but feel
as easing in our bones, like sleeping cold
and someone tucks us in. It's an old

song of the comfort of giving comfort, told
by the wood-burning stove that warmed our bones
five months while the sun backed off, a song
for March's sparseness where we walk our dogs

through elms and oaks with no leaves on, past
slants of light like silvered walking sticks.
On such a cleanly beaming morning, is it
any wonder we think our trees are singing?

II.

We pry a deer bone from the hound's mouth,
a slobbery job, and wedge it high in the crotch
of a sassafras, stashing possible death
where we can see it, but the dogs can't.

These messy meddlings get to be a habit:
more and more we walk our dogs past
other morning's purloined bones clacking
in branches like prayer wheels. Lacking

faith in fate, we let our dogs ramble, then
whistle them back, as if wildness
could be tethered, as if our little forest's
orders and bounds were set in place by us

each time we walk these woods, still winter-bare
today except where plums and dogwoods flower
as pink as skin among the oaks and poplars
greening themselves awake with mindless ease.

KATHERINE WILLIAMS

The Shot

The puppy I just watched get run over and I are in the garden seeing if
the lettuce seeds have sprouted yet. She sniffs at the dirt and says "Nope.
Another day or two." Together she and I grab one end of a stick and Louie
takes the other in his chops and the three of us race around the yard. With
the puppy who lit out from under the vintage Indian bike on a crushed leg,
I go check the mail. No mail. She runs circles around me as I head back
toward my house. At her house there's nobody home. She is at the shelter
getting morphine and her squashed belly assessed by a vet. Then she starts
digging up a place near my trash can. I ask her if she is scared or lonely
there, and she says to throw her the ball. She says to let her in the bed with
me because there's frost on the ground. She laps up a big drink of water
with her fast little tongue and says she hopes the guy on the bike is okay,
and I say "Well, he's pretty mad but he'll get over it. Some gash on his
helmet," I tell her, "You don't mess around." We sit on the sofa watching
Making It Grow. I rub her face, so ugly it's cute. She says she's just got to
chase bikes, it's a genetic thing. At the shelter the vet gives her The Shot.
As I pull new weeds out of the garden I hold her in my lap, gently because
she's so badly damaged. She licks the earthy sweat of my hand, drowsily.

Hand

I
My body and your body and our body.
The two-fingered hand.

II
She never follows the four winds,
only the fifth—the cyclone—
wind of the fist.

III
Tracer of love in the dust.
Spike in the tree.
Bringer of madness.

IV
Two hands interlace, not ours.
It is a charcoal of my other hands.

V
The hand fumbles at cats cradle in sunlight:
it takes far longer
when there are eyes involved.

VI
Key to the dialect of midnight:
the vowels are always shaped
like fingers.

VII
Even narcissists hold their breath
at the sound of those hand-shadows
parting the air.

VIII
Morning seeped in under the door
as blue fog. Four hands
cradled the steam above one clay mug.

IX
Marionettes danced
the Firebird across the stage
as though their souls were fingers.

X
Not painting, but the act of painting
—the presence of the absent hand.

XI
How is the piano without hands
like a painting without speech?

XII
With a wave of the Leader's hand,
hundreds were lost.

XIII
One glimpse of the cosmos is forever.
When read like braille,
the stars sizzle in the hand.

WILLIAM WRIGHT

Night, Yonce's Field

I am in Carolina,
fixed in a dark cathedral
of flowers. Oh Lord,
the night roads
snake the fields, coldly:

All the girls I've loved
sleep warmly
in the foxfire of dreams,
married, raced off
toward oblivion. God,

if I am to be
the stranger keen
to a ripe word's madness,
then blend deep autumns
in my hands.

Dreaming of My Parents

They are in a hotel somewhere
in France, the room smelling
of ancient books. A hickory tree
taps against a window
where light pours golden,
as in Vermeer. My God,
how beautiful they are,
together again.

I cannot believe
his delight in smoothing
her hair with an ivory comb,
the strokes meticulous
and delicate, as if she were
a fragile doll cherished
through the centuries.

Taking his rough feet
as if they were wingless
birds, she caresses them, lowers them
into steaming soap-water,
washes them with a touch so focused
that I have no choice
but to witness.

Here They Are, Beautiful and Alone

They are in an old boat near the heart
of Lake Greenwood, a breeze helping them home.
Bream splash the surface under a dusk
fainting to violet, a Carolina postcard. Tentative, my parents
are new lovers, stunned in the beginning
of affection. For moments they are perfectly still,

transfixed statues, love trembling behind their eyes
and aching with something like joy.
Now I dream for them a purity deep as the leaves
he rows her through, the oak and elm rinsed in soft words.

Here they are, beautiful and alone
in each other's world: He paddles to dockside
and leads her up through sweet gum and birch,
trails through dark leaves.

Radio towers glow and fade
like numbed hearts long after love's first gimmick,
the same sad rhythm of an old wife's hands
kneading dough at a kitchen sink, full of regret.

Look at them, he says, pointing to their red beacons;
*there won't be any stars tonight, Sandy, but the towers
try their best.* She loves them like a young girl,
basking in his effort to perfect the scene.

Clouds roll near: The smell of rain
weighs down the wind. Retiring
to the lake-house bedroom, they undress,
make love as the storm ticks the tin roof.

I am made on this night. I want to believe
their embrace was anything
but indifferent, was slow, measured,
that pleasure was between them.

It will be years before they refuse to touch each other,
when soft summer rains finally wilt them down,
drowning their tenderness, when stars and towers
fade like hearts of fire, empty promises,
and the lake is merely a place
both yearn to forget.

TOMMY SCOTT YOUNG

My Wild Beautiful Bird

i put her in a gilded cage
so from my favorite seat to muse
admiring her brilliant color

i expected her to sing

instead she stared at a painting
of hills and trees and birds in the wild
as her feathers drooped to fade

her silence was an eerie sound

i moved her by a window
where the morning sunlight streams
bringing the joy of day and seasons

i expected her to sing

silently she stared into the distant sky
far beyond change and light and time
deep into a purple midnight blue

her melancholy permeated my dreams

weeping in the dark, i was
in sleepwalk wandering aimless
empty, from room to room

i expected to sing

but transported in magical arms of Morpheus
one morning i found myself by an open window
she was sitting on the sill

her silence was an eerie sound

she looked at me with gratitude
then swiftly away she flew
easy landing in a nearby tree

wrestling with noise she battled

flitting lithely from limb to limb
as from silence to sonance she sorted sound
until wondrous song filled the wind

silence was an eerie sound

stretching and mighty lifting high
i saw my wild beautiful bird
disappearing in the distant sky

Deserted

i look left
& rails & crossties
lined by bright white
& deep blue lights
disappear
to a fine point
centered in pitch black

i look right
& rails & crossties
lined by bright white
& translucent green lights
disappear
to a fine point
fading in stark pale yellow

i see no trains

Breathing Easy

many times you slept
gently curled in my arms
breathing easy on the F line
speeding through dark watery tunnels
between that twenty four dollar island
and a cost of millions Prospect Park
we traveled to 15th street north
past nowhere, near everywhere
Sometimes you knitted pieces
to a long red scarf with faint traces
of your soul and your sweet perfume
symbol of a never to be broken bond
a perfect friendship circle of string
i admired your fingers and your toil
the love you transferred to each thread
and though time has swiftly melted
long days and bottomless empty years
I still see your every perfection
your every beautiful flaw
deeply hidden in a watery
secret place of timeless memory
and as I pause I sometimes think
maybe you were a mermaid
in a half forgotten dream

THE POETS

DAN ALBERGOTTI's poems have appeared in *Ascent, Meridian, Mid-American Review, Prairie Schooner, The Southern Review, The Virginia Quarterly Review,* and other journals. He was a Tennessee Williams Scholar at the 2003 Sewanee Writers' Conference, a fellow at the Virginia Center for the Creative Arts in July 2004, and the Richard Soref Scholar in Poetry at the 2004 Bread Loaf Writers' Conference. His *Charon's Manifest* won the 2005 Randall Jarrell/Harperprints Chapbook Competition, and one of his poems was reprinted in *Best New Poets 2005.* His poem "Things to Do in the Belly of the Whale" won the 2005 Oneiros Press Poetry Broadside Contest and will be printed in a limited letterpress edition in late 2006. A graduate of the MFA program at UNC Greensboro and former poetry editor of *The Greensboro Review,* he currently serves as associate poetry editor of *storySouth* and teaches at Coastal Carolina University in Conway, SC.

GILBERT ALLEN has lived in Travelers Rest, SC, since 1977. His books of poems are *In Everything, Second Chances, Commandments at Eleven,* and *Driving to Distraction.* With Bill Rogers, he co-edited the anthology *A Millennial Sampler of South Carolina Poetry* in 2005.

PAUL ALLEN teaches poetry writing and writing song lyrics at The College of Charleston in Charleston, SC. Published in numerous journals and anthologies, his work includes *American Crawl* (Vassar Miller Poetry Prize, UNT Press, 1977) and the chapbook *His Longing: The Small Penis Oratorio* (Foothills Publishing, Kanona, NY, 2005), a sequence of metaphysical conceits. He has also produced a CD of poems and songs, *The Man with the Hardest Belly,* available on Napster.

KEN AUTREY teaches English at Francis Marion University in Florence, SC. His poems have appeared in *The Chattahoochee Review, Cimarron Review, The Devil's Millhopper, Hubbub, Interim, Poetry Northwest, South Carolina Review, Tar River Poetry, Texas Review,* and other magazines.

JAN BAILEY is the 2003 winner of the Elinor Benedict Poetry Prize from *Passages North* and the Sue Saniel Elkind Poetry Prize from *Kalliope.* A SC Arts Commission Poetry Fellow and Pushcart Prize Nominee, she is the author of three collections, the most recent *Midnight in the Guest Room* (2004). She is the former department chair in creative writing at the SC Governor's School for the Arts and Humanities.

FRAN BARRETT is a SC native who studied Telecommunication Arts and Creative Writing at the University of Georgia. She currently lives in Charleston, where she is a pre-school teacher and travels with the Charleston Poetic Jazz Society as a featured poet. Her credentials also include readings/performances in the Piccolo Spoleto Poetry Sundown Series and Monday Night Blues.

FREDERICK BASSETT's poems have appeared or are forthcoming in *Apostrophe*, *Negative Capability*, *Passanger*, *Pembroke Magazine*, *Plainsongs*, *Potato Eyes*, *Pudding Magazine*, *The Cape Rock*, *The Savannah Literary Journal*, and *Zone 3*. He also has poems anthologized in *A Millennial Sampler of South Carolina Poetry*, edited by Gilbert Allen and William Rogers (Ninety-Six Press 2005). Paraclete Press has published two books of "found" poems that he arranged from Biblical lyrics—*Love: The Song of Songs* and *Awake My Heart*.

MICHAEL BASSETT was born and raised in Upstate SC. He earned an MFA in poetry from Vermont College and has recently completed the Ph.D. in poetry at the University of Southern Mississippi. His poetry has won the Joan Johnson award and the Fugue Fourth Annual Poetry Contest, judged by Tony Hoagland. Pudding House Press published his chapbook, *Karma Puppets*, in 2003.

CLAIRE BATEMAN teaches at the Fine Arts Center in Greenville, SC. She is the author of five books: *The Bicycle Slow Race* (Wesleyan); *At the Funeral of the Ether* (Ninety-Six Press); *Friction* (Eighth Mountain Press); *Clumsy* (New Issues Poetry and Prose), and *Leap* (New Issues Poetry and Prose).

LIBBY BERNARDIN, a SC Arts Commission's literary fellow (1986-87), is a retired English teacher who published her novel, *The Stealing*, in 1993. Her poems have been published in several journals, including *Notre Dame Review*, *The Devil's Millhopper*, and *Negative Capability*. Most recently, her poem "Spirit" was a finalist in the Poetry Initiative contest of *The State Newspaper*. The poem "Nameday" won honorable mention in the Porter Fleming contest in 1994. She was on the SC Arts Commission 1990 Reader's Circuit, and, until accepting a full-time faculty position at USC, she served for a number of years in the arts-in-the-schools program. She has worked as a reporter for *The State*, and was editor of the *Palmetto Banker*, a statewide banking magazine. She served on the Board of Governors of the SC Academy of Authors for five years.

LAUREL BLOSSOM's most recent book of poetry is *Wednesday: New and Selected Poems* (Ridgeway Press 2004). She has been honored with fellowships from the NEA, the New York Council on the Arts, and the Ohio Arts Council, among others. Her work has been nominated for the Pushcart Prize and has appeared in a many anthologies and journals including *Poetry*, *The American Poetry Review*,

Pequod, The Paris Review, and *Harper's.* She co-founded the esteemed writing residency and workshop program, The Writer's Community, and now serves as chair of the Writers Community Committee of the YMCA National Writer's choice. She lives in Edgefield, SC.

CATHY SMITH BOWERS is the author of three collections of poetry: *The Love That Ended Yesterday in Texas* (Texas Tech University Press, 1992), *Traveling in Time of Danger* (Iris Press 1999) and *A Book of Minutes* (Iris Press 2004). Her poems have appeared widely in such publications as *The Atlantic Monthly, The Georgia Review, Poetry, The Southern Review,* and *The Kenyon Review.* She has received The General Electric Award for Younger Writers, the SC Arts Commission Fiction Project, and the SC Arts Commission Poetry Fellowship. She served for many years as poet-in-residence at Queens University of Charlotte where she received the 2002 JB Fuqua Distinguished Educator Award. She now teaches in the Queens low-residency MFA creative writing program.

FARLEY BRIGGS was born in Florence, SC, and attended the University of South Carolina in Columbia. While a student there she won two first prizes from The Poetry Society of South Carolina. More recently her poems have been published in *The Best of Sand Hills, Kennesaw Review* and *Poetry of the Golden Generation.* She has done freelance creative writing workshops anywhere from Augusta State University's Kids College to the Augusta Medical Correctional Institution.

STEPHEN COREY is the author of ten poetry collections, most recently *There is No Finished World* (White Pine Press 2003), *Greatest Hits, 1980-200* (Pudding House Publications 2000), *Mortal Fathers and Daughters* (Palanquin Press 1999), and *All These Lands You Call One Country* (University of Missouri Press 2002). His poems, essays, articles, and reviews have appeared in *The American Poetry Review, Poetry, The Kenyon Review, The New Republic, The North American Review, Ploughshares, Yellow Silk, Shenandoah, Poets & Writers, The Ohio Review, The Virginia Quarterly Review, The Laurel Review,* and elsewhere. Since 1983 Corey has been on the editorial staff of *The Georgia Review.* Associate editor since 1986, he is currently acting editor . In 1976 he co-founded *The Devil's Millhopper,* for which he was co-editor and then editor until 1983.

ROBERT CUMMING has received a poetry fellowship from the SC Arts Commission and a Fulbright-John F. Kennedy Fellowship to teach and translate contemporary poetry in Thailand. His work has appeared in two anthologies of South Carolina poetry (*45/96: The Ninety-Six Sampler of South Carolina Poetry* and

Twenty: South Carolina Poetry Fellows) and in magazines including *The Chattahoochee Review*, *Southern Poetry Review* and *The Sow's Ear*. Cumming has taught at Lander University, the City College of New York, Thammasat and Silpakorn Universities in Bangkok. He now lives in Davidson, North Carolina.

PHEBE DAVIDSON is the author of several collections of poems (most recently *Song Dog* from the SC Poetry Initiative and *The Drowned Man* from Finishing Line Press). Her work has appeared in a large number of journals and magazines, including *Southern Poetry Review*, *Kenyon Review*, *Asheville Poetry Review*, *Main Street Rag* and *The South Carolina Review*. A new chapbook, *Twelve Leagues In*, is forthcoming from Spire Press. Recently retired from several lifetimes of teaching and academic work, she lives in Westminster, SC, with her husband Steve and their cat Fripp. Retirement, in Davidson's view, rocks.

KWAME DAWES was Born in Ghana in 1962 and spent most of his youth in Jamaica. He is profoundly influenced by the rhythms and textures of that lush and complex place, citing in a recent interview his "spiritual, intellectual, and emotional engagement with reggae music." His book *Bob Marley: Lyrical Genius* remains the most authoritative study of the lyrics of Bob Marley. His 11th and 12th collections of verse, *Wisteria: Poems From the Swamp Country* and *Impossible Flying* were published in 2006, as were his reflections on living in America, *A Far Cry from Plymouth Rock: A Personal Narrative* He is Distinguished Poet-in-Residence at the University of South Carolina and programming director of the annual Calabash International Literary Festival in Jamaica.

KEN DENBERG is the editor of the Snail's Pace Press and has poems in *Agni*, *Southern Poetry Review*, *Sundog*, *The Comstock Review*, *Denver Quarterly*, *Shenandoah*, and *The New York Quarterly*. The author of *Driving with One Light Out* (The Devil's Millhopper Press, 1993), he was the 2005 New York State Council on the Arts Literature Fellow.

CURTIS DERRICK lives with his wife and daughter in Columbia, SC, where he teaches at Midlands Technical College. He has also taught for the Johns Hopkins University's Center for Talented Youth (CTY), for which he designed the poetry tutorial. Through CTY's Distance Education Program, he has mentored young poets from across the continental US, as well as Europe, Asia, and the Middle East.

SKIP EISIMINGER is a student of the late James Dickey, who advised "Cast a wide net." Eisiminger is the author of *Wordspinner* (word games), *The Consequence of*

Error (essays), *Non-Prescription Medicine* (poems), and *Omi and the Christmas Candles* (children's book).

JAMES ENELOW, a southern boy, was raised between Georgia and South Carolina, and has pursued his education in Louisiana and Texas. He currently understands that the summer heat gets worse the further west you go. His work has appeared in *The New Review, The Review, River King Poetry Supplement*. While pursuing his Ph.D. at the University of Texas at Dallas, he revamped the literary journal *Sojourn*.

EDWIN C. EPPS is a National Board Certified teacher at Spartanburg High School in Spartanburg, SC. He is the author of *Literary South Carolina* (Spartanburg: Hub City Writers Project 2004) and the former editor of *South Carolina Writing Teacher*. His poetry has appeared in *POINT, The Savannah Literary Journal, Drift*, the anthologies *Out of Unknown Hands* and *Rhythms, Reflections, and Lines on the Back of a Menu*, and elsewhere. He is currently at work on a baseball book to be called *Beautiful Duncan Park: A Father and Son Explore a Classic American Ballpark*.

LINDA ANNAS FERGUSON *is* the author of four collections of poetry. Her third chapbook, *Stepping on Cracks in the Sidewalk*, was released from Finishing Line Press (2006) and a full book, *Bird Missing from One Shoulder*, is forth-coming from WordTech Editions (June 2007). She was the 2005 Poetry Fellow for the SC Arts Commission and served as the 2003-2004 Poet-in-Residence for the Gibbes Museum of Art in Charleston, SC. Her work is featured in the anthologies *Twenty: South Carolina Poetry Fellows, A Millennial Sampler of South Carolina Poetry*, and the 2006 *Kakalak Anthology of Carolina Poets*.

JOAN FISHBEIN's work has appeared in *The Devil's Millhopper, Helicon Nine, The Best of Sand Hills, The Kennesaw Review*, and assorted other small literary magazines.

STARKEY FLYTHE, JR. lives in North Augusta, SC. He has published two poetry collections, both from Furman's Ninety-Six Press, and was the winner of the Iowa prize for short fiction for *Lent: The Slow Fast*. He has lately been studying Arabic with the Egyptian writer Emad Francis, renewing an interest from time spent in the military.

CHRIS FORHAN, originally from Seattle, lived in Charleston from 1989-1999. The poems included here were written during his time in South Carolina and appeared in his first book, *Forgive Us Our Happiness*, which won the 1998 Katherine Bakeless Nason Prize. His second book, *The Actual Moon, The Actual Stars*, won the Samuel French Morse Prize and the Washington State Book Award. His work has also won a Pushcart Prize and been published in *Poetry*, *Paris Review*, *New England Review*, and other magazines. He teaches at Auburn University.

RICHARD GARCIA has lived in Charleston, SC, for three years. He is the author of two books of poetry, *The Flying Garcias* (University of Pittsburgh Press) and *Rancho Notorious* (BOA Editions, Ltd.) His next book of poetry, *The Persistence of Objects*, is forthcoming from BOA in October, 2006. Recent work of his appears in *The Notre Dame Review*, *The Georgia Review*, *Crazyhorse* and *Ploughshares*. He is the recipient of a Pushcart prize, and a poem of his is included in *Best American Poetry 2005*.

STEPHEN GARDNER, a recovering academic dean, is G. L. Toole Professor of English at USC Aiken, where he has taught poetry and creative writing for thirty-five years. His poems, fiction, essays, and critical articles have appeared widely in such venues as *Southern Review*, *Poetry Northwest*, *Connecticut Review*, *Texas Review*, *Cimarron Review*, *Southern Poetry Review*, and *California Quarterly*. He served as editor of both *kudzu* and *The Devil's Millhopper* magazines and is the author of *This Book Belongs to Eva*.

GEORGE P. GARRETT, author and editor/co-editor of over fifty books, is an icon in the literary landscape who has made an indelible mark in poetry, fiction, non-fiction and, some would even say, in screen-writing. During his four-decade teaching career, he helped shape the lives—both literary and human—of generations of aspiring writers. His numerous awards and honors include the Rome Prize from the American Academy of Arts and Letters, fellowships from the Ford, Guggenheim, and Rockefeller foundations, as well as from the National Endowment for the Arts. In addition to serving as Poet Laureate of the state of Virginia, he has received the Aiken Taylor Award for Modern American Poetry, an Award in Literature from the American Academy of Arts and Letters, and the PEN/Malamud Award for Excellence in Short Fiction. Now retired from the University of Virginia, where he held the Henry Hoyns Chair of Creative Writing, he lives in Charlottesville with Susan (also an excellent writer), his wife of over fifty years.

CECILE GODING is from Florence, SC, where she worked in neighborhood adult literacy programs for some years. She attended Furman University and Francis Marion University, and received a poetry fellowship from the SC Academy of Authors. Her poetry chapbook, *The Women Who Drink at the Sea*, was published by State Street Press. Goding currently lives in Iowa City, Iowa, where she attended the University of Iowa's Program in Nonfiction Writing and the

Writers' Workshop in Poetry. Her poems have appeared in *The Devil's Millhopper*, *The Georgia Review*, *Poetry Northwest*, *Weaving Magazine*, and other journals.

VERA GÓMEZ attended the University of Iowa's Summer Writer's Workshop and was an integral part of the Greenville Poetry Slam Teams (1997-98) that won Southeast Regional Competition and competed nationally. A performance poet/writer, Gómez currently teaches social studies/language via poetry through an arts integration program and has coordinated the Emrys "Reading Room" series. In 2004, she facilitated a "Young Voices" high school poetry/art workshop with the Greenville County Museum and has twice been named a finalist in the SC Poetry Initiative's Poetry Contest. A native Texan, born to immigrant parents, Gómez strives to balance her written and oral poetry with her first generation, Mexican-American female voice. A Texas Tech University graduate, she has worked in television media, at Clemson University, and for an Internet travel site. Currently, Gómez works in corporate communications and calls Greenville, SC, home.

ALY GOODWIN's work been published in *Bayleaf*, *The Iowa Review*, *Appalachian Heritage*, *Davidson College Miscellany*, *Unaka Range*, *Concept*, *A Millennial Sampler of South Carolina Poetry*, and others. In 2002 she was recipient of James Larkin Pearson Award from the Poetry Council of North Carolina. In 2004 she placed second in the Hub City Writers Project poetry contest.

LAUREN GOULD has lived in Charleston, SC for three years and now attends North Carolina State University in Raleigh, North Carolina.

LINDSAY GREEN received her MA in American Literature from the University of South Carolina, where she is currently finishing her Ph.D. in Composition and Rhetoric. She teaches Composition, Advanced Composition, and Business Writing at USC. For the last six years, Green has been teaching poetry to young adults in and around Columbia. She has performed with several dance companies in the past sixteen years and is presently a member of The Power Company in Columbia.

BEN GREER has published five novels, the most recent of which was released by Texas Review Press in 2006. His sixth novel, also by Texas Review Press, will be published in the fall of 2007. Recently, he has been publishing poetry. He teaches at the University of South Carolina.

LINDA LEE HARPER has received four Pushcart nominations and three Yaddo fellowships. She has published six collections of poetry, most recently *Blue Flute*

(Adastra Press). Her work has appeared in over 80 literary journals in the US, Europe and Canada, including *The Georgia Review, Nimrod, Rattle,* and *Southern Humanities Review*, where she won the Hoepfner Award for Best Poem of the Year. She resides in Batesburg-Leesville, SC, and Augusta, GA, where she never plays golf.

MELANIE GAUSE HARRIS received the Ph.D. in American Literature from the University of South Carolina. Her awards include two Academy of American Poets Prizes, The Frank Durham Creative Writing Award, *The Devil's Millhopper* Kudzu Prize, a SC Fiction Project Award and The SC Academy of Authors Fellowship in Poetry. Her work has appeared in such publications as *From the Green Horseshoe: The Poems of James Dickey's Students, 45/96: The Ninety-Six Sampler of South Carolina Poetry, The Blue Unicorn, The South Carolina Review, Iris, Kalliope, The State Newspaper,* and *The Wall Street Journal*. Dr. Harris is now a visiting professor of English at Charleston South-ern University and a member of the board of the SC Academy of Authors.

MARGARET B. HAYES has been published in several periodicals, among them, the South Carolina Writers Workshop anthology, *Horizons,* in Anderson College's literary magazine, *Ivy Leagues,* in *The Writers News and Guidelines* in Sarasota, Florida, in the newspaper, *Gwinnett Post,* Lawrenceville, Georgia. She is a native of SC.

JANNETTE HYPES is a lazy poet and SC native living among the beautiful hills of east Tennessee with her husband, daughter, and cats. She is the two time recipient of the James Oswald Creative Writing Award and the 2000 winner of the Libba Moore Gray Poetry Competition. Her poetry has been published by the *Snail's Pace Review, The Clark College Writers Workshop* and in *Breathing the Same Air: An East Tennessee Anthology* (Celtic Cat Publishing).

THOMAS L. JOHNSON recently retired as librarian emeritus and English instructor from USC in Columbia. He is an award-winning poet and co-editor of two photographic collections (*A True Likeness* 1986; *Camera Man's Journey* 2002). For many years he edited the poetry page in the Columbia newsmonthly *Point.* He now lives in Spartanburg, SC, where he serves on the board of directors of the Hub City Writers Project.

ANGELA KELLY was awarded the SC Fellowship of the Arts from The SC Arts Commission in 1999. She is author of three poetry chapbooks, most recently *weighing the body back down,* winner of the Tennessee Chapbook Prize (Middle

Tennessee State University 1996). She has had individual poems published in numerous journals, including *North American Review, Nimrod, The Asheville Poetry Review, Slipstream, Kalliope, Rhino, Inkwell, Rosebud,* and *Rattle.*

JOHN LANE's writing has been published in several volumes of poetry, including *Quarries, As the World Around Us Sleeps, Against Information and Other Poems, The Dead Father Poems,* and *Noble Trees.* He has three books of essays, including two, *Waist Deep in Black Water* and *Chattooga,* from The University of Georgia Press. He teaches at Wofford College in Spartanburg, SC, and is a cofounder of The Hub City Writers Project.

THOMAS DAVID LISK lived in Sumter, SC, for 15 years before moving to Raleigh, NC. His recent work has appeared in *Massachusetts Review, Hotel Amerika, Bat City Review, Jacket,* and *Borderlands.* He is a six-time nominee for the Pushcart Prize. His published poetry collections are *A Short History of Pens Since the French Revolution* and *Aroma Terrapin. These Beautiful Limits* is forthcoming from Parlor Press in 2006.

SUSAN LUDVIGSON'S seventh book with LSU Press is *Sweet Confluence: New and Selected Poems* (2000), and she has a new book forthcoming: *Escaping the House of Certainty.* Others from LSU are *Trinity, Everything Winged Must Be Dreaming,* and *To Find the Gold.* Among the journals in which she has published poems are *The Atlantic Monthly, The Nation, The Paris Review, Virginia Quarterly Review, Ohio Review, Gettysburg Review,* and *The Georgia Review.* She publishes essays on the arts in literary magazines and in the photography journal *21ˢᵗ.* Her awards include a Rockefeller-Bellagio fellowship and grants and fellowships from the NC Arts Council and the SC Arts Commission. She has represented the US at writers' congresses in France, Belgium, Canada, and Yugoslavia and given poetry readings in those countries and throughout the U.S., including at the Library of Congress. Since 1975 she has taught at Winthrop University in Rock Hill, SC.

ED MADDEN is associate professor of English at the University of SC and poet in residence at the Riverbanks Botanical Gardens in Columbia. His chapbook *Signals* won the 2005 SC Poetry Initiative's contest and was published in 2006. Madden is a two-time recipient of the SC Academy of Authors fellowship in poetry, and he was selected in 2006 as an artist in residence for the SC State Park system. His poems have been published in many journals, including *College English, Los Angeles Review, River City, Solo, Southern Humanities Review,* and *James White Review,* as well as in the collections *Gents, Bad Boys, and Barbarians: New Gay Male Poetry* and *A Millennial*

Sampler of South Carolina Poetry. His poems are also included in a forthcoming Notre Dame anthology of Irish-American Poetry from the 18th century to the present. Madden grew up on a soybean and rice farm in rural Arkansas.

REBECCA MCCLANAHAN's most recent book is a collection of memoir-based essays, *The Riddle Song and Other Rememberings*, which won the 2005 Glasgow. She has also published four volumes of poetry (most recently *Naked as Eve*) and three books about writing, including *Word Painting: A Guide to Writing More Descriptively*. Her work has appeared in *The Best American Essays, The Best American Poetry, Ms. Magazine, Georgia Review, Gettysburg Review, Boulevard,* and numerous anthologies; it has also been aired on NPR's "The Sound of Writing," "Living on Earth" and "The Writer's Almanac." McClanahan's awards include a Pushcart Prize in fiction, the Wood prize from *Poetry*, a New York Foundation for the Arts Fellowship in nonfiction, and (twice) the Carter prize for the essay. She lives in New York City and teaches in the low-residency MFA program at Queens University, Charlotte; the Kenyon Review Writers Workshops; and the Hudson Valley Writers Center. *Deep Light: New and Selected Poems* 1987-2007 is forthcoming from Iris Press in 2007.

TERRI MCCORD has published poetry in journals such as *Seneca Review, Cimarron Review,* and *Cream City Review.* The SC Arts Commission awarded her the 2002 poetry fellowship. Recent awards include a *South Carolina Review* honorable mention, a finalist in the 2006 *Southeast Poetry Review* contest, a finalist in *The State* 2006 contest, and a 2005 Southern Artistry Award. Her work is also included in the Hub City Press anthology *Twenty: South Carolina Poetry Fellows.* McCord earned her MFA from Queens University in Charlotte.

KEN MCCULLOUGH's most recent poetry books are *Obsidian Point* (2003) and *Walking Backwards* (2005), as well as a book of stories, *Left Hand* (2004). He has received numerous awards for his poetry, including the Academy of American Poets Award, a National Endowment for the Arts Fellowship, a Pablo Neruda Award, a Galway Kinnell Poetry Prize, the New Millennium Poetry Award, the Blue Light Book Award and the Capricorn Book Award. Most recently, he received grants from the Witter Bynner Foundation for Poetry, the Iowa Arts Council, and the Jerome Foundation to continue translating the work of U Sam Oeur. *Sacred Vows*, a bilingual edition of U's poetry with McCullough's translations, was published in 1998. U's memoir, *Crossing Three Wildernesses*, was co-written with McCullough and published in 2005. McCullough lives in Winona, Minnesota, with his wife and younger son and works at St. Mary's University of Minnesota.

RAY MCMANUS received his MFA in poetry (2000) and Ph.D. in Composition and Rhetoric (2006) from the University of South Carolina. His poetry has appeared in *Crazyhorse*, *Nimrod*, *Natural Bridge*, and many other journals throughout the US and Canada. He teaches creative writing, composition, and business writing at USC. He is Writer in Residence for the Palmetto Center for the Arts and Creative Writing Director for the Tri-District Arts Consortium. His book of poetry, *driving through the country before you were born*, will be published by USC Press in 2007.

MAURINE MELECK's poetry has appeared in many journals, including *Calliope* and *Luna Negra*. She writes and paints in North Augusta, SC, and lives with her 8 year old grandson, whom she hopes to recover from autism. She is an active member of the autism community.

SUSAN MEYERS is the author of *Keep and Give Away* (University of South Carolina Press 2006), selected by Terrance Hayes for the SC Poetry Book Prize. Her chapbook, *Lessons in Leaving*, was selected by Brendan Galvin for the 1998 Persephone Press Book Award. Her poems have appeared in numerous literary journals, as well as on the websites Poetry Daily and Verse Daily. A long time writing instructor, she lives with her husband in the rural community of Givhans, near Summerville, SC.

RICK MULKEY is the author of four poetry collections including *Toward Any Darkness* (Word Press 2006), *Before the Age of Reason* (Pecan Grove Press 1998) and two chapbooks, *Bluefield Breakdown* (Finishing Line Press) and *Greatest Hits: 1994-2003* (Pudding House Press). Individual poems and essays have appeared in such journals as *Denver Quarterly*, *The Literary Review*, *Poetry East*, *Connecticut Review*, *Poet Lore*, *Shenandoah*, and in several anthologies, including *American Poetry: The Next Generation*, *Poems and Sources*, and *A Millennial Sampler of South Carolina Poetry*. His awards include a Hawthornden Fellowship for a writing residency in Scotland, and the Charles Angoff Award in poetry from *The Literary Review*.

ROBERT PARHAM's work has been accepted for publication or published by *Southern Review*, *Georgia Review*, *Shenandoah*, *Connecticut Review*, *Northwest Review*, *Apalachee Review*, *Asheville Poetry Review*, *Rattapallax*, *Southern Humanities Review*, *Atlanta Review*, *Weber Studies*, *South Carolina Review*, *Cimarron Review*, *Notre Dame Review* and many other journals. His chapbook *What Part Motion Plays in the Equation of Love* won the Palanquin Competition. A collection of his poetry was a finalist for the Richard Snyder and the Marianne Moore poetry competitions. He presently edits the *Southern Poetry Review* and serves as Dean of the Katherine Reese Pamplin College of Arts and Sciences at Augusta State University.

JIM PETERSON's poetry collections include *The Man Who Grew Silent* (Bench Press 1989); *Carvings on a Prayer Tree* (Holocene Press 1994), *An Afternoon With K* (Holocene Press 1996); *The Owning Stone* (Red Hen Press 2000, winner of the Benjamin Saltman Award), and *The Bob and Weave* (Red Hen Press 2006). His novel *Paper Crown* was published by Red Hen Press (2005). Peterson received a Poetry Fellowship from The Virginia Arts Council in 2003. His work has been published widely in such journals as *Poetry, Georgia Review, Shenandoah, Prairie Schooner, Poetry Northwest,* and *Texas Review.* His plays have been produced in regional and college theatres. He is currently Coordinator of Creative Writing at Randolph-Macon Woman's College in Lynchburg, VA, where he lives with his wife Harriet and his beloved Welsh Corgi, Dylan Thomas. His dog is better looking than he is, but Harriet doesn't really care, because she loves snouts.

ELLEN RACHLIN's *Waiting for Here* was published by Finishing Line Press (2004). Her poems have appeared in such journals as *American Poetry Review, Confrontation, The Comstock Review, White Crow, North Atlantic Review, Links, San Miquel Writer, The Pointed Circle, Wings Online, prechelonian, The Iconoclast,* and *Poetry Motel.* Born in Buffalo, NY, educated at Cornell University (AB), The University of Chicago (MBA) and Antioch University (MFA in creative writing), she lives in New York City, works in finance, and serves as treasurer of the Poetry Society of America.

RON RASH holds the John Parris Chair in Appalachian Studies at Western Carolina University. He is the recipient and winner of many awards, including an NEA Poetry Fellowship (1994), the Sherwood Anderson Prize (1996), the Novella Festival Novel Award (2001) and Foreword Magazine's Gold Medal in Literary Fiction (2002) for his novel *One Foot in Eden,* which was also named Appalachian Book of the Year. His 2005 novel *Saints at the River* was named Fiction Book of the Year by both the Southern Book Critics Circle and the Southeastern Booksellers Association. His poetry and fiction have appeared in over one hundred journals, magazines and anthologies, including *The Longman Anthology of Southern Literature, Sewanee Review, Yale Review, Georgia Review, Kenyon Review, New England Review, Southern Review, Shenandoah* and *Poetry.* His other books include *The Night The New Jesus Fell to Earth* (short stories), *Casualties* (short stories), *Eureka Mill* (poetry), *Among the Believers* (poetry), and *Raising the Dead* (poetry). In 2005 he received the James Still Award from the Fellowship of Southern Writers. His third novel, *The World Made Straight,* was published by Henry Holt in 2006.

ALEX RICHARDSON is assistant professor of English at Limestone College where he teaches creative writing, modern poetry, Shakespeare and film. He earned a

Ph.D. from the Center for Writers at the University of Southern Mississippi. His poems have appeared in numerous magazines and journals. He was the alternate for the SC Poetry Fellowship in 2004, and his manuscript, *Spending the Night*, was a finalist in the National Poetry Series Open competition.

HARRIET POPHAM RIGNEY's poetry has been published in *Another Chicago Magazine* and *Confrontation* in addition to the *Eureka Literary Magazine* and *Red Rock Review*. Her work won two prizes from the Poetry Society of SC this year. Her first ancestor in Charleston arrived in 1688 and lived diagonally across the street from where Rigney now lives. She has been an editor of popular fiction for many years, including a stint as founding Editorial Director of Tor Books. Rigney is married and has one son, one cat, and many goldfish.

LEE ROBINSON grew up in Columbia, SC, and practiced law in Charleston for more than 20 years. Her novel, *Gateway*, was published by Houghton Mifflin in 1996. She is a three-time winner of the SC Arts Commission's Fiction Prize. Her poems and essays have appeared in many journals, and her poetry collection, *Hearsay*, chosen by Robert Wrigley as the winner of the 2004 Poets Out Loud Prize, was published by Fordham University Press and received the Violet Crown Award from the Writers League of Texas. Lee now lives on a ranch in the hill country of Comfort, Texas, with her husband, Jerry Winakur, and teaches at the Center for Medical Humanities and Ethics at the University of Texas at San Antonio.

JEAN-MARK SENS lives in Thibodaux, LA, where he is Collection Development Librarian at Nicholls State University and teaches culinary classes at the John Folse Culinary Institute. Born in France and educated in Paris, he has lived in the American South for over fifteen years, taught English at Rust College, the University of Mississippi, and the University of South Carolina. He holds the MLIS from USC as well as degrees in English from the University of Southern Mississippi and Paris VII University. He also holds an Associate in Science in Culinary Arts from Johnson & Wales. He has published poems in various magazines in the US and Canada. Red Hen Press in California published his first collection *Appetite* in the Fall 2004

WARREN SLESINGER, after graduating from the Iowa Writers Workshop with an MFA, taught English part-time while working full-time in the publishing business as an editor, marketing manager or sales manager at the university presses of Chicago, Oregon, Pennsylvania, and South Carolina. He received an Ingram Merrill grant (1971) and an SC Arts Commission Poetry Fellowship

(2003). Slesinger's poetry has appeared in *The American Poetry Review, The Antioch Review, The Beloit Poetry Journal, Cimarron Review, The Georgia Review, The Iowa Review, New Letters, The North American Review, North West Review, Poetry Daily, The Sewanee Review*, and *The South Carolina Review*.

BRIAN SLUSHER teaches English, public speaking, and drama at Westside High School in Anderson, SC. His poetry has appeared in such magazines as *Flyway, Free Lunch, Poem, The Southern Poetry Review*, and *Yemassee*. A selection of his poems is included in the books *Quintet* and *A Millennial Sampler of South Carolina Poetry* (both Ninety-Six Press), and the South Carolina Poetry Initiative published his chapbook *Waking in the Driver's Seat* in 2006. A graduate of Furman University, he lives with his wife Terri McCord in Greenville, SC.

CHARLENE SPEAREN received her MFA in poetry from the University of South Carolina in 2003, where she is currently working on her Ph.D. in Composition in Rhetoric. She is the Program Coordinator for USC's Arts Institute and Assistant Director for the SC Poetry Initiative. She is Poet in Residence for both the Columbia Museum of Art and Trinity Episcopal Cathedral. Her poetry has been published in *Yemassee, Writers at Carolina, Aspects*, and *Promise Magazine*. She was the 2005 first place winner for the *Be the Voice in the Dark* Poetry Contest and the 2000-2001 co-winner of the James Dickey Award for poetry.

LAURA STAMPS is an award-winning poet and novelist. Over seven hundred of her poems, short stories, and poetry book reviews have appeared in literary journals, magazines, anthologies, and broadsides, including *Louisiana Review, The Pittsburgh Quarterly, Poetry Midwest, Big City Lit, Poesy Magazine, American Writing*, and the *Chiron Review*. The recipient of a Pulitzer Prize nomination and six Pushcart Award nominations, she is the author of more than thirty books and chapbooks of poetry and fiction. Recent books include *The Year of the Cat* (Artemesia Publishing 2005) and *The Cat Lady: A Novel in Verse* (Kittyfeather Press 2006).

DAVID STARKEY, after receiving his MFA from Louisiana State University in 1990, lived in Florence, SC from 1990-95, and taught English at Francis Marion University. While there, his work was anthologized in *45/96: The Ninety-six Anthology of South Carolina Poetry*. Over the past eighteen years he has published more than 400 poems in literary magazines around the world; his latest collection is *Ways of Being Dead: New and Selected Poems* (Artamo 2006). He is co-author, with Wendy Bishop, of *Keywords in Creative Writing* (Utah State 2006) and editor of *Living Blue in the Red States* (Nebraska 2007). Starkey is currently at work on an introductory creative writing textbook for Bedford/St. Martin's.

SUSAN FINCH STEVENS often incorporates her poems into mixed-media visual pieces and artist's books. Her poetry has appeared in the anthology *Kakalak* and is forthcoming in the anthology *In the Yard*. She was the 2003 poet-in-residence at the Gibbes Museum of Art and has participated in numerous readings and exhibits in the Charleston area. She and her husband live on the Isle of Palms.

DENNIS WARD STILES grew up on a small dairy farm in northern Illinois. After graduating from the U.S. Air Force Academy in 1964, he served thirty years in the Air Force as a pilot and military diplomat. He spent much of his career overseas, with assignments or accreditation in Thailand, South Vietnam, England, Iceland, France, Egypt, the Sudan, Austria, Slovenia and Slovakia. He has published widely in journals and has four chapbooks to his credit: *Saigon Tea* (Palanquin Press 2000), *Black Mirrors* (Pudding House Publications 2003), *Spit* (The Poetry Society of SC, winner of the Kinloch Rivers competition 2004) and *A Strange Wind Rises* (Pudding House Publications 2006). He has served twice as president of the Poetry Society of SC and is a former Poet in Residence at the Gibbes Museum of Art. He lives in Charleston with his wife Mary Jane.

SHEILA TOMBE was born in Belfast, Northern Ireland, and has studied in Scotland, Spain, and the US, receiving her Ph.D. in Comparative Literature from the University of South Carolina in 1993. She has taught English in Spain and Spanish in Japan, but now she is an associate professor of English at USC Beaufort, where she specializes in Shakespeare. Her work has appeared in *Poetry Without Borders* (Gival Press 2005), *A Millennial Sampler of South Carolina Poetry* (Ninety-Six Press 2005), *Rosebud, Yemassee, Fortnight* (Northern Ireland), and elsewhere.

DENO TRAKAS is Professor of English and Director of the Writing Center at Wofford College. He has published fiction and poetry in magazines such as *The Denver Quarterly* and *Oxford American*. He's also published two chapbooks of poetry and is working on two novels and a book on Greeks of the Upstate in South Carolina.

RYAN G. VAN CLEAVE's most recent books include *The Magical Breasts of Britney Spears* (Pavement Saw 2004) and a creative writing textbook, *Contemporary*

American Poetry: Behind the Scenes (Allyn & Bacon/Longman 2003). He lives in upstate SC.

CEILLE BAIRD WELCH is profiled in Edwin Epps' *Literary South Carolina* (2004). Much of Welch's poetry is written for equity performance. Holding degrees in psychology and counseling from the University of South Carolina, Welch was awarded the honorary Dr. of Arts from Lander University for "literary accomplishment and patronage of the Arts." Her poetry has been performed throughout the Southeast and is included in *A Millennial Sampler of South Carolina Poetry* (2005). Also a dabbler in short fiction, Welch is a multiple winner of The SC Fiction Project and The Spoleto Fiction Open and has contributed to the short story anthology, *Inheritance* (2001).

MARJORY WENTWORTH was born in Lynn, Massachusetts. Educated at Mt. Holyoke College and Oxford University, she received her MA in English Literature and Creative Writing from New York University. Her poems have appeared in numerous books and magazines, and she has twice been nominated for The Pushcart Prize. *Nightjars*, a chapbook of her poems, was published by Laurel Publishing (1995). Recently, her poems have been published with Mary Edna Fraser's art in a book of poetry and monotype prints, *What the Water Gives Me*. *Noticing Eden*, a collection of poems, was published by Hub City Press (2003). She serves on the Board of Directors of the Southern Literature Council of Charleston and lives in Mt. Pleasant, SC, with her husband Peter and their three sons. She is the Poet Laureate of South Carolina.

DANA WILDSMITH grew up in south Georgia, the daughter of a Methodist minister who was active in working for social justice. She attended college wherever her Navy husband's career took them, finally obtaining a B.A. in Sociology from Virginia Wesleyan College. In 1999, she returned to her family's land in north Georgia, where she and her extended family work to preserve a 125-year-old family farm in the midst of encroaching development. In 1992, Wildsmith was named a Poetry Fellow of the SC Academy of Authors, and her second chapbook, *Annie*, won the Palan-quin Press competition.. Her most recent book, *One Good Hand*, was a SIBA Poetry Book of the Year nominee and has been nominated for Appalachian Book of the Year. Her poems and essays have been widely published in such journals *Yankee, Kentucky Poetry Review*, and *Chattahoochee Review*.

KATHERINE WILLIAMS, while running UCLA's transgenics facility, studied poetry with Cecilia Woloch, David St. John, and her husband Richard Garcia;

she authored three chapbooks and gave readings throughout Southern California. She is published in various anthologies and has received a Pushcart nomination. She now lives on James Island, near where she grew up, and studies Caribbean corals at the Hollings Marine Laboratory.

WILLIAM WRIGHT was born in 1979 and reared in Edgefield, SC. His award-winning first full collection of poems, *Dark Orchard*, was published in 2006 by Texas Review Press. Recent work has appeared or is forthcoming in *North American Review, Nimrod, Texas Review, Cimarron Review, Borderlands, Phoebe, Poet Lore, storySouth*, and *Pacific Review*. He is co-editor of the multi-volume *Southern Poetry Anthology* as well as several forthcoming volumes. Founder and editor of *Town Creek Poetry*, he is a Ph.D. student and Excellence fellow in the University of Southern Mississippi's Center for Writers.

TOMMY SCOTT YOUNG, a storyteller, poet, playwright, author, producer, teacher, and sculptor, was born in Blair, SC. He received his B.A. degree from California State University at Los Angeles. He also pursued graduate work in sculpturing. Young is best known in SC for his founding and directing the Kitani Foundation, which from 1977 to 1983, was a leader in bringing nationally acclaimed performing artists to SC. His books include *Tommy Scott Young Spins Magic Tales, Black Blues and Shiny Songs*, (poetry); and *Crazy Half Sings a Crazy Wolf Song*. He currently resides in New York City, where he is a Storyteller-in-Residence at the Lincoln Center Institute.

ACKNOWLEDGEMENTS

Except where specifically noted, all poems in this anthology are used by permission of the author. Poems not listed in these acknowledgements have not been published previously.

DAN ALBERGOTTI: "The Chiming of the Hour" originally appeared in *The Southern Review* (Spring 2006). "Revision" originally appeared in *Virginia Quarterly Review* (Fall 2005). "Things to Do in the Belly of the Whale" originally appeared in *Southern Humanities Review* (Spring 2001) and was reprinted in *Charon's Manifest* (NC Writers' Network 2005).

GILBERT ALLEN: "The Noah of Travelers Rest" originally appeared in *The Southern Review* (Summer 1998) and was reprinted in *Driving to Distraction* (Orchises 2003). "Fearful Symmetry" originally appeared in *Shenandoah* (Spring 2005). "Lunch in the Park" originally appeared in *Poetrybay* (Summer 2005).

PAUL ALLEN: "Ground Forces in the Academy" and "The Drive Home after the Hearing" originally appeared in *The Southern Review*, vol. 41, no. 3 (2005). "He Loses Focus in His Lecture on 'A Good Man Is Hard to Find'" first appeared in *His Longing: The Small Penis Oratorio* (Kanona, NY: Foothills Publishing 2005).

KEN AUTREY: "Still Life with Piranhas" originally appeared in *Alligator Juniper*, vol. 20 (2004).

JAN BAILEY: "With What Wild Hand" first appeared in *Passages North*, vol. 25, no. 1 (2004), then was included in *Midnight in the Guest Room* (The Leapfrog Press 2004) and in *Twenty, South Carolina Poetry Fellows* (Hub City Writers Project, 2005). Breath appeared in *Southern Poetry Review*, 42:2 (2003).

FREDERICK BASSETT: "Women Who Plow" originally appeared in *Pembroke Magazine*. "Goat Rock" originally appeared in *Apostrophe*. "Rock Springs Churchyard" originally appeared in *The Cape Rock*.

MICHAEL BASSETT: "Awakenings" originally appeared in *Concho River Review*. "Something About the Way She Touches" originally appeared in *Barrow Street*. "Slugs" originally appeared in *Publications of the Mississippi Philological Society*.

CLAIRE BATEMAN: "Distinction," "How We Fall," and "Reprieve" were published in *Clumsy*, © Claire Bateman, 2003. Reprinted with permission from New Issues Poetry and Prose.

LIBBY BERNARDIN: "Spirit" originally appeared in *The State* newspaper (Columbia, SC).

LAUREL BLOSSOM: "Morbid Fascination" originally appeared in *Caprice* and is included in *Wednesday: New and Selected Poem* (Ridgeway Press 2004). "The Papers Said" originally appeared in *The New York Quarterly* and is included in *The Papers Said* (Greenhouse Review Press 1993). "How Can I Tell" originally appeared in *The Papers Said*.

STEPHEN COREY: "The Blooming of Sentimentality" and "Past, Present, Future" were previously published in *All These Lands You Call One Country* (University of Missouri Press 1992). "The Ugly Stepsisters" was previously published in *The Last Magician* (Water Mark Press 1981; reissued by Swallow's Tale/Livingston Press 1987).

PHEBE DAVIDSON: "Staying Cool," "Broad Daylight," and "Up Long Cane" were all originally published in *Song Dog*, a winner of the SC Poetry Initiative's 2005 chapbook competition (South Carolina Poetry Initiative 2006).

KWAME DAWES: "Brother Love" originally appeared *Impossible Flying* (Peepal Tree Press 2006).

KEN DENBERG: "Baby, It's Cold Outside" originally appeared in *Poems & Plays*, no. 10. "Blueberry Pie" originally appeared in *Agni Review*, no. 36. "Kiss Me" originally appeared in *The Comstock Review* (vol. 17, no. 2).

JAMES ENELOW: "Manhattan Transfer" originally appeared in *New Review*, vol. 3, no. 3 (1996).

LINDA ANNAS FERGUSON: "Living Room, 1956" originally appeared in *Last Chance to Be Lost* (Kentucky Writers' Coalition). "Choices " originally appeared in *Skirt Magazine*. "The First Night" originally appeared in *The Georgia Poetry Society: Seventy-Fifth Anniversary Edition*.

CHRIS FORHAN: "O.K. Fine," "A Sickly Child," and "The Vastness. The Distant Twinkling" were previously published in *Forgive Us Our Happiness* (University Press of New England 1999).

RICHARD GARCIA: "These Moments" originally appeared in *Ecotone*, vol. 1, no. 2. "The White Ghosts" originally appeared in *The Georgia Review*, vol. LIX, no. 4. "Eradication of Exotic Pests" originally appeared in *Blackbird*, vol. 4, no. 2.

STEPHEN GARDNER: "Waiting to Leave" originally appeared in *The Cimarron Review*, #44 (July 1978).

GEORGE P. GARRETT: "Shards for Her" originally appeared in *Mademoiselle*, vol. LVII, no. 4 (August 1963). It was subsequently reprinted in *For a Bitter Season* (University of Missouri Press 1967), *The Collected Poems of George Garrett* (University of Arkansas Press, 1984), and in *Days of Our Lives Lie in Fragments: New and Old Poems, 1957-1997* (LSU Press 1998). "Giant Killer" was published in *The Sleeping Gypsy and Other Poems* (University of Texas Press 1958) and was reprinted in *The Collected Poems of George Garrett* and *Days of Our Lives Lie in Fragments*. "Gray on Gray" first appeared in *kudzu* (no. 9, Spring 1979) in a slightly different form and was reprinted in *Luck's Shining Child* (Palaemon Press Limited 1981).

CECILE GODING: "Yankee Doodle" was originally published in *The Georgia Review* (Summer 1992).

VERA GÓMEZ: "Cafeteria Food" was originally published in *Millenial Sampler: South Carolina Poetry Anthology* (Ninety-Six Press 2005).

MELANIE GAUSE HARRIS: "In Yellowstone Park, Fires Burn out of Control" was originally published *The South Carolina Review* (Fall 1989).

THOMAS L. JOHNSON: "The Artist's Subject" was originally published in *Spirit of Place* (Charleston, SC, 1998). "The Grave of Abdul Aziz al-Saud" was originally published in the *Poetry Society of South Carolina Yearbook* 1991). "A Southern Boy Reflects on Miss Monroe" was originally published in *Pearl* (Fall/Winter 1990) and is reprinted here with permission from *Pearl*.

SUSAN LUDVIGSON: "The Lilies of Lansford Canal" was previously published in *Sweet Confluence* (LSU Press 2000). "Barcelona, the Spanish Civil War: Alfonso Laurencic Invents Torture by Art (which previously appeared in *Poet Lore*) and "Bin Laden in South Carolina" (which previously appeared in *Gettysburg Review*) were both reprinted in *Escaping the House of Certainty* (LSU Press 2006).

ED MADDEN: "Light" was originally published, in an earlier version, in the *Los Angeles Review*. Both "Light" and "Cabin, Near Caesar's Head" were published in *Signals* (SC Poetry Initiative 2006).

REBECCA MCCLANAHAN: "Ex-Brother-in-Law" was originally pub-lished in *Poetry*. "Hello Love" was first published in *The Gettysburg Review*." "Traveling" was first published in *Boulevard*." All three of these poems were reprinted in *The Intersection of X & Y* (Copper Beech Press 1996).

TERRI MCCORD: "Metering" was originally published in *A Millennial Sampler of South Carolina Poetry* (Ninety-Six Press 2005). "Principle of Uncertainty" was originally published in *Seneca Review* (Spring 2006).

RAY MCMANUS: "Red Barn" was originally published in *Nimrod* (Spring/ Summer 2003).

SUSAN MEYERS: "Someone Near Is Dying" was originally published in *Southern Poetry Review*. "Guitar" was originally published in *Crazyhorse*, "Neither the Season, Nor the Place" was originally published in *The Southern Review*. These three poems are reprinted from *Keep and Give Away*, published by the University of South Carolina Press, 2006. Used by permission of University of South Carolina Press.

RICK MULKEY: "Insomnia" was originally published in *The Literary Review* and was reprinted in *Verse Daily* and in *Greatest Hits 1994-2003* (Pudding House Press); it will also be reprinted in *Toward Any Darkness* (Word Press 2006). "Blind-Sided" was originally published in *The Southern Poetry Review* and was reprinted in *Before the Age of Reason* (Pecan Grove Press). "Why I Believe in *Angels*" was originally published in *Before the Age of Reason*.

JIM PETERSON: "Alive and Well at the Camelback Inn" was originally published in *Mid-American Review* (Fall 1982) and was reprinted in *The Man Who Grew Silent* (The Bench Press 1989). "The Man Who Grew Silent" was originally published in *From the Green Horseshoe: Poems by James Dickey's Students* (USC Press 1987) and was reprinted in *The Man Who Grew Silent* (The Bench Press 1989). It has also been reprinted in *The Art and Craft of Poetry* (Writers Digest Books 1994) and *Jim Peterson's Greatest Hits* (Pudding House Publications 2001 & 2003). "The Owning Stone" was originally published in *The Georgia Review* (Summer 1998). It was reprinted in *The Owning Stone* (Red Hen Press 2000) and *Jim Peterson's Greatest Hits* (Pudding House Publications 2001 & 2003).

ELLEN RACHLIN: "Radishes in Childhood" was previously published in *Waiting for Here* (Finishing Line Press 2004), online in *Addenda: Bearing Life* (2004); and it is pending publication in *Beyond*, edited by Rochelle Ratner, forthcoming from Red Hen Press. "Crocuses was originally published in *Waiting for Here*. Both poems are reprinted here with permission from Finishing Line Press.

RON RASH: "Bloodroot" was originally published in *Shenandoah*." "Shadetree" was originally published in *The Southern Review*." "The Reaping" was originally published in *The Sewanee Review*.

ALEX RICHARDSON: "Hammock" originally appeared in *White Pelican Review*, vol. 5, no. 1 (2004).

HARRIET POPHAM RIGNEY: "Prothalamion for Jones" was originally published in *Red Rock Review*. "Song" was originally published in *Eureka Literary Magazine*.

WARREN SLESINGER: "The Ring of Dancers" was originally published in *The Sewanee Review* and was reprinted in *Twenty: South Carolina Poetry Fellows* (Ninety-Six Press). "Fog" was originally published in *The State* (Columbia, SC) newspaper. "Never Simple or Still" was originally published in *The Iowa Review*.

BRIAN SLUSHER: "The Drunken Couple" was originally published in *Waking in the Driver's Seat* (Stepping Stones Press 2006).

CHARLENE SPEAREN: "Portals," "Her Muteness Grew Louder and Louder," and "Tree Climber" were originally published in *Without Possessions* (Stepping Stone Press 2006), the Press' first issue for its Editor's Choice series.

LAURA STAMPS: "Eight Zonal Geraniums" was originally published in *Song of the San Joaquin*.

DAVID STARKEY: "The Argument" was originally published in *Hubbub*. "Try a Little Tenderness" was originally published in *Poetry East*. Both poems are forthcoming in *Ways of Being Dead: New and Selected Poems* (Artamo 2006).

DENNIS WARD STILES: "Mother" was originally published in *The Poetry Society of South Carolina Yearbook* (2005).

SHEILA TOMBE: "Borges on the Internet" was originally published in *Rosebud Magazine* (October 2000).

DENO TRAKAS: "Zelda," "The Smaller House," and "After Reading Your Dead Father Poems" were previously published in *human and puny* (Holocene Press 2000). "Zelda was also published in *45/96: The Ninety-Six Sampler of South Carolina Poetry* (Ninety-Six Press). "After Reading Your Dead Father Poems" and "The Smaller House" were also published *A Millennial Sampler of South Carolina Poetry* (Ninety-Six Press 2005).

RYAN G. VAN CLEAVE: "The Kudzu Queen" previously appeared in *Illuminations*, no. 21 (August 2005).

MARJORY WENTWORTH: "The Last Night" was originally published in *The Beloit Poetry Journal* (Fall 1991). "Homecoming" was originally published in *75: Retrospective of the Poetry Society of South Carolina* and was subsequently reprinted in *Noticing Eden* (Hub City Writers Project 2003).

DANA WILDSMITH: "Ambience" and "Bones" were previously published in *One Good Hand* (Iris Press 2005) and are reprinted here by permission of The Iris Publishing Group. "Cautionary" was previously published in *Our Bodies Remember* (Sow's Ear Press 2000).

WILLIAM WRIGHT: "Night, Yonce's Field" was originally published in *Pacific Review*, vol. 23 (2005). "Here They Are, Beautiful and Alone" was originally published in *Poet Lore*, vol. 99, no. 1/2 (Spring/Summer 2004). "Dreaming of My Parents" was originally published in *Texas Review*, vol. XXIV, no. 1 & 2 (Spring/Summer 2003). These poems were reprinted in *Dark Orchard*, winner of the *Texas Review* Breakthrough Poetry Prize (Texas Review Press 2006) and are reprinted here with permission from Texas Review Press.